The Endless Steppe

with Connections

The Endless
Steppe

Esther Hautzig

with Connections

HOLT, RINEHART AND WINSTON
A Harcourt Education Company
Austin • Orlando • Chicago • New York • Toronto • London • San Diego

For permission to reprint copyrighted material, grateful acknowledgment is made to the following sources:

HarperCollins Publishers: The Endless Steppe by Esther Hautzig. Copyright © 1968 by Esther Hautzig.

Dial Books for Young Readers, an imprint of Penguin Putnam Books for Young Readers, a division of Penguin Putnam Inc.: From *Summer of My German Soldier* by Bette Greene. Copyright © 1973 by Bette Greene.
Doubleday, a division of Random House, Inc.: From *The Diary of a Young Girl: The Definitive Edition* by Anne Frank, edited Otto H. Frank and Mirjam Pressler, translated by Susan Massotty. Copyright © 1995 by Doubleday, a division of Random House, Inc.
Golden Ink: From "The Trail of Tears" from *About North Georgia,* accessed November 12, 2001, at http://ngeorgia.com/history/nghisttt.html. Copyright © 1996, 1997 by Golden Ink.

The New York Times Company: From "Gorbachev, Last Soviet Leader" by F. Clines from *The New York Times,* December 25, 2000. Copyright © 2001 by The New York Times Company.

Cover Illustration: Philip Howe/Deborah Wolfe Ltd. Based on original cover art by HarperCollins.

ISBN 978-0-03-067527-0

15 16 17 18   1083   15 14

4500495704

Contents

The morning it happened—the end of my lovely world —I did not water the lilac bush outside my father's study.

The time was June 1941 and the place was Vilna, a city in the northeastern corner of Poland. And I was ten years old and took it quite for granted that all over the globe people tended their gardens on such a morning as this. Wars and bombs stopped at the garden gates, happened on the far side of garden walls.

Our garden was the center of my world, the place above all others where I wished to remain forever. The house we lived in was built around this garden, its red tiled roof slanting toward it. It was a very large and dignified house with a white plaster façade. The people who lived in it were my people, my parents, my paternal grandparents, my aunts and my uncles and my cousins. My grandfather owned the house, my grandmother ruled the house; they lived rather majestically in their own apartment, and the rest of us lived in six separate apartments. Separate, but not exactly private. There were no locked doors: people were always rushing in and out of each other's apartments to borrow things, to gossip, to boast a bit or complain a bit, or to tell the latest family joke. It was a great, exuberant, busy, loving family, and heaven for an only child. Behind the windows looking out on our garden there were no strangers, no enemies, no hidden danger.

Beyond the garden, beginning with the tree-lined avenue we lived on, was Vilna, my city. For the best view of Vilna one went to the top of Castle Hill, and I was always asking Miss Rachel, my governess, to take me there. Built along the banks of the river Wilja in a basin of green hills, Vilna has been called a woodland capital. It was a university town, a city of parks and white churches with gold and red towers built by Italian architects in an opulent baroque style, a city of lovely old houses hugging the hills and each other. It was a spirited and a gay city for a child to grow up in.

From this hilltop I could make out the place where my family's business took up half a block, the synagogue we attended, the road that led to the idyllic lake country where we had our summer house. When I stood on this hilltop everything was just as it should be in this best of all possible worlds, my world.

And, down to the smallest detail, I would not have had any of it changed. What I ate for breakfast on school mornings was one buttered roll—a soft roll, not a hard roll—and one cup of cocoa; any attempt to alter this menu I regarded as a plot to poison me.

I would sit down to this breakfast at a round table in the dining room with my young parents or my beloved

Miss Rachel. My father—called Tata, the Polish for papa—was my most favorite person in the world, a secret I thought I ought to keep from Mama. Tata was gay and fun-loving and not only made jokes himself, but laughed at mine—whether mine were funny or not.

Mama was gay, too, with an engaging talent for laughing over spilled milk, but at an early age I found out that she was a strong-minded lady who thought that one indulgent parent was quite enough for an only child. When I was four years old, she and I first locked horns. I had just begun to attend a progressive nursery school, and one morning, when I and a dozen or so other little girls were doing calisthenics on the floor, I made a shattering discovery. All legs had been swung back over heads, all toes were touching the floor, when, rolling my eyes from side to side, I saw that all the panties thus displayed were silk—white, pink, blue, yellow silk, a gorgeous rainbow of silk panties, some even edged with lace—except mine. Mine were white cotton, severely unadorned. I told Mama that this situation must be corrected immediately. She thought not. I said that if I could not wear silk panties I would not go to nursery school at all. Mama said: "Very well. Don't go." I didn't go; I stayed home until it was time for me to go to grade school when I was seven.

And when it came to choosing the school, Mama decided it was character-building for a rich child to go to a school where there were children from all economic brackets. I went to the Sophia Markovna Gurewitz School, where I learned Yiddish and was introduced to the literature and culture of my people.

I loved school and I loved the order of my life. My

3

days were planned with the precision of a railroad schedule. On Mondays after school there were piano lessons; Tuesdays, dancing class; Wednesdays I went to the library and invariably argued with the librarian, who recommended children's books when I wanted grown-up books, particularly mysteries and the more blood-curdling the better. On Thursdays my cousins and I had calisthenics with a muscular lady who drilled us as if we were candidates for the Prussian Army, which made us explode into giggles. And on Fridays I was allowed to help Mama and the cook prepare the Sabbath meals—braid the *challah*, the ritual bread, and chop the noodles. On Fridays, the seven kitchens of our house would send forth the marvelous smells of seven Sabbath meals all alike—the same breads, sponge cakes, chickens, and chicken soup.

But in 1939 Hitler's armies marched on Poland.

When the first bombs fell over Vilna I was terrified, of course. But we were lucky; no bombs fell in our garden. Our garden was invulnerable.

To be sure, there were changes.

Tata was drafted into the Polish Army to fight the German invaders. But Mama assured me that he would come back. She continued to do so in the face of considerable evidence to the contrary. And since I had great faith in Mama, I believed her. I was the only one who did.

Shortly after Tata left, word came that his entire battalion had been wiped out. Our family was stricken with a deep and inconsolable grief. Everyone, that is, except Mama and me. Mama told them to stop their weeping, that Tata was alive. They looked up from their grief and begged her to come to her senses and accept the dreadful reality. They understood that this aberration came from her great love for her husband, but when she went so far as to have a fight with the rabbi about it, they were beside themselves.

On a Monday morning, Mama woke up and announced to anyone who would listen to her that Tata would be back in Vilna on Thursday. She advised everyone to stop weeping and prepare for his return. "Be sure to get me some farmer's cheese, the kind he adores," she said to her poor mother, who now wept not only for the lost son-in-law, but for the daughter gone crazy. Mama herself had our house shined up from top to bottom and our larder stocked with Tata's favorite foods.

On Thursday, Tata returned, just as Mama had predicted. But by way of preparing everyone for the surprise, he stopped at his mother-in-law's house first. My grandmother opened the door, took one look at this "ghost" and screamed: "Oh, dear Lord, I didn't get the cheese."

At eight, I took Mama's psychic powers for granted.

Over and over Tata told us how he had walked from village to village, after his battalion was disbanded. The few men who had survived were told to make their way home as best they could. Dressed in a blanket and with a beret on his head, pretending he was mad, Tata had had many narrow escapes before he came back to us.

He was home, but in the next two years there would be other changes. In 1940 the Russians, who were then allied with Germany, occupied Vilna. They confiscated the family business and our property, but did not evict

5

us from our house, our garden. The servants left and Miss Rachel got married. One didn't always have small luxuries, but I didn't miss them.

My world was still intact and I had not the slightest premonition that it was about to end.

The morning it happened I awakened very early for a reason. Since school was over I was allowed to sleep late. Naturally, in order to enjoy such a special privilege one had to be awake.

The minute I opened my eyes and saw my pink and white curtains fluttering in the soft breeze blowing off the Wilja, I knew it was going to be a beautiful day, a perfect June day. Heeding our family tradition, I was careful to slip out of bed with my right foot forward. Right foot forward, good luck for the day; left foot forward, bad luck. In Poland, one listened to one's family if one wanted good luck.

I went to the window to see if Grandfather was in the garden. This garden was the pride and joy of his life. It was he who gave the gardeners their orders, scolded when a tree had not been properly pruned, was lavish with his praise when an ailing plant was saved. "Remember, children," he would say to my cousins and me, "remember that there is always some good in people who love flowers."

That morning, Grandfather was not in the garden. But I leaned out the window for a minute to admire the roses and the peonies and the lilac bush which I would water in an hour or two I thought.

It must have been about six o'clock.

I picked up the mystery I had been saving for just such a morning, and went back to bed with it. From the opening sentence, I was lost to the rest of the world. Hence, I heard nothing.

I was well into the book when my mother burst into the room.

"You must get up immediately," she said, stripping the bedclothes off me.

"But why? Mama——" I was outraged.

"Esther, for once do as you're told without asking questions. Quickly!"

I jumped out of bed.

"Mama—what is it?"

"Questions, always questions. Keep your voice down." She had dropped hers to a whisper. "Esther—something is happening. Uncle David called. He said—he said that Russian soldiers were swarming all over Grandfather's apartment. Your father rushed there. He didn't even stop to dress. He's still in his pajamas. And he isn't back yet. Please get dressed as fast as you can and come right to my room."

Russian soldiers! I didn't argue; I did as I was told, braiding my hair as I went. I found my mother sitting on her bed with a large kitchen-match box on her lap. What on earth was Mama planning to do with matches in her bedroom? And why was she looking at me so oddly? Could she be frightened?

"You are to take this box to my mother's house, Esther, to your Grandmother Sara. Immediately."

"A match box? To Grandmother Sara? Whatever for?"

"Esther!" Her voice was trembling. "Stop asking questions! Just do as you're told. Take this box to your grandmother. I have a feeling we won't be needing what

I've put inside. I want Grandmother to have it. You are to leave by way of the garden gate. Don't go out on the street. Go through the alleys. Go quickly and come back as quickly as you can. Do you hear me? You are not to linger at your grandmother's, not for one extra minute."

I almost dropped the box.

"Esther—" Mama's voice became gentle "—Esther, I'm sorry that I was cross but—oh, do hurry, for God's sake, hurry!"

I was scared. More scared than I had been when Vilna was being bombed. Even a child soon learns what bombing is all about, learns to know what *might* happen, and to be relieved when it doesn't. But now I didn't know what was happening. I didn't know how to say my prayer, how to bargain with God. One needed to be explicit, I thought as a child—"Dear God, please do not let the bomb fall on the Rudomin house on Great Pogulanka Avenue in Vilna. If you will be kind enough to see that this doesn't happen, I promise that I will *try* not to talk back to my mother tomorrow. . . ." I had tried to bargain fairly during the German bombings in 1939. But now I couldn't pray. There was no dark bomb shelter, no lap in which to bury my face when the bomb was too close, no soothing words from Mama to ease the terror of glass breaking and bricks falling.

I ran through my father's study into the garden. The minute I crossed the door, I knew I had made a mistake. I had put my left foot forward. I wanted to go back and start over again with the right foot, but I was afraid to waste time. As I ran, I touched the lilacs and inhaled their fragrance. I would water them later. The garden had not changed; my garden was just as beautiful, just as safe as always. As if there were nothing to threaten my life in it, it would be waiting for me when I returned from this bewildering errand. I went to the back gate and out into the alley.

I flew through the alley. Mercifully, it was deserted that morning. Running as fast as I could, within ten minutes I was at the apartment house where my grandmother lived. But once there, I did have to stop to catch my breath before I could climb the stairs two at a time.

There was no answer to my first ring, nor to my second. I pounded on the door with the heel of my shoe. Finally my grandmother's sleepy voice called out, "Who is it?"

"Me, Grandmother. Let me in."

She opened the door and began firing questions at me: Why was I visiting so early? Why was I out of breath? What was in the box? I wanted to shout at her the way my mother had: No questions! I don't have the answers! Instead, I told her what I knew, that soldiers were in Grandfather Solomon's house, that Tata went there in his pajamas. "In his pajamas?" she asked, as if this were the most terrifying fact of all. Yes, in his pajamas, I repeated, beginning to react to this with terror myself.

I handed her the box and when she opened it we both gaped.

My mother's emeralds and other jewels were lying there in that kitchen-match box—her necklace, earrings, and all her rings. They looked so strange lying there out of their velvet boxes, like play jewelry.

My grandmother closed the box. She shut her eyes and her lips moved in prayer.

"Grandmother. I must go, Grandmother. Mama said I must come back quickly. Grandmother—? I guess Mama had a reason for sending you her jewelry—?"

She went on with her praying. I stood on tiptoe and kissed her on the cheek. I hugged her and rested my cheek against her arm. I longed to tell her how much I loved her, how much she meant to me, how well I remembered all the days she spent with me when I was little, cutting out paper dolls and building cardboard houses. But there was no time. I could only manage to say, "I love you, Grandmother, I love you so much."

"Oh, my child—tell your mother—"

She broke off and kissed the top of my head.

"I will see you soon, Grandmother," I said as I ran out the door.

As I ran down the stairs, a terrible thought came to me: I would never see my grandmother again. Oh, God, please don't let me have such terrible thoughts, I prayed.

I ran all the way home. When I reached the garden door, I could hear the front-door bell ringing and ringing. Where was Mama?

My mother was sitting in the dining room, at the empty dining table, resting her chin in her hand.

"Mama, the doorbell is ringing. Don't you hear it? Shall I open the door?"

"No. I'll open it myself." But she still didn't move. "Sit down, Esther. You're out of breath. Did you give the box to Grandmother?"

"Of course I did. Mama—the doorbell—"

"Yes, the doorbell."

She rose slowly and, taking a long time to get there, she opened the door.

My father was on the doorstep, his hands behind his back. Next to him stood two Russian soldiers with fixed bayonets.

Not one word was spoken. Father and Mother exchanged a guarded look, but Father kept his eyes away from me, as if he was ashamed to have me see him in pajamas with bayonets at his back. Slowly and silently, Father walked through the hall, past the umbrella stand with his walking sticks, into the dining room. The soldiers walked heavily beside him. When they reached the center of the room, the silence was broken. One of the soldiers shouted:

"Down on the floor! All of you! You're under arrest!"

Clearly, before we would do such a silly thing, my father would explain everything and the soldiers would go away. He had not done anything wrong—neither stolen, nor killed anyone, nor committed any other crime— they could not arrest him. He would insist that they apologize. But he remained silent. We sat on the floor —first my father, then me. For a second, I thought my mother would refuse to. My father must have thought so too because he murmured her name softly: "Raya—" Very awkwardly, but determined to keep her back straight, my mother sat down on the floor too.

How could we be arrested without having done anything wrong? I decided to find out.

"Why are we under arrest?" I asked.

My mother lifted an admonishing hand, but it was too late.

The soldiers looked from me to my suddenly very pale parents and then at each other. The one who had issued the order had bright little eyes and an extraordinarily broad nose; it was he who pulled out a long white paper and read from it.

" ' . . . you are capitalists and therefore enemies of the people . . . you are to be sent to another part of our great and mighty country . . .' "

The soldier read on and on, the words seeming to pour out of his huge nostrils—so many words and so dull. Most of them were incomprehensible to me. What was a capitalist? The only words that meant anything to me were the ones that were bringing my world to an end. I was to be taken from my home, from the city where I was born, from the people I loved. I didn't feel like an enemy of the people, only an enemy of these horrid soldiers. I hated them. Loathed them. Despised them. I wished they were dead.

My mother reached out and tried to straighten my clenched fingers. "I am fine, Mama, really I am," I said, more to reassure myself than her.

The soldier stopped reading; he seemed quite satisfied that he had performed his duty admirably, and he refolded the paper as if it were a very precious document.

My mother spoke quietly. "Esther, you will go to your room and gather your clothes together."

I didn't move. Was there to be no argument? no pleading? no miraculous adult intervention?

My mother nudged me and we both scrambled up from the floor. When my father said he would help my mother pack their things and began to get up too, the other soldier tilted his bayonet toward Father and said: "Don't move. Stay where you are." My father obeyed, but now he held his head in his hands.

When I reached my room, I started to close my door. "Leave that door wide open, girl," the soldier shouted.

I did. I walked into my room and looked around. This was my room: my curtains were blowing in the breeze; my wallpaper continued to sprout its tiny rosebuds; my dolls were in their customary huddle on the divan; my books were on the shelves; the mystery I had been reading lay face down on the bed. No, I would not leave this room. No one could make me. I would will myself to fall down dead in a little heap on the floor before I would leave it.

When that didn't work, I wanted to throw myself down on the bed and howl. But the door was open and the soldiers were out there. Whether from fear or bravado I cannot say, but I held my tears back and began to pack.

What clothes would one need in that "other part of our great and mighty country"? My light oak wardrobe was filled with skirts and blouses and school uniforms and party dresses. Left to myself, I was happiest in a pair of old shorts and a shirt. This brought me close to tears again; shorts and shirt meant fun and freedom, carefree days in the country, holidays at the sea. I picked up the albums of family photographs, the record of days with my family—picnics with aunts and uncles and cousins in the woods, bathing in the sea, baby pictures, birthday parties, the photographs of the grownups in what we children called their clothes of olden times, the ones that sent us into fits of giggles. At once, this album became my most important possession and I put it down on the bed along with some books, including the unfinished mystery.

The album called something to my attention, something very strange indeed. The house was quiet, much too quiet. Where was everyone? I tiptoed to the window overlooking the garden. Where was Uncle David? and Aunt Bertha? and Aunt Sonia? Where *were* they? The garden was quiet and deserted; no voices, no laughter from the windows.

I went back to the wardrobe with a dreadful feeling . . . not fright, not anger, something nameless and worse.

I gathered some clothes together and dumped them on the bed.

In the dining room, my father still sat on the floor. His shoulders sagged and he looked up at me with dull, unseeing eyes. Within a single morning, on a perfect June day, my young father had become an old man. Looking down at my father, I deliberately ignored the soldiers and their authority to tell me what I might and might not do—and asked for my father's permission to go to my mother. He nodded and patted my hand.

My mother too had changed. Usually she was composed and fastidiously groomed, but now her face was flushed and her beautiful crown of braids was tumbling down. Her huge mahogany wardrobe and her bureaus, normally in immaculate order, were in wild disarray. Dresses had slipped off their hangers and lay crumpled on the floor; lingerie spilled out of drawers. My mother was feverishly piling clothes on the bed, zigzagging from bureaus to the wardrobe to the bed. I asked her for something to do; I had finished gathering my things and wanted desperately to be busy. Doing nothing was too frightening.

"Go ask your father. Can't you see I'm busy?" She hid her face from me and I knew she was close to tears. Tears were against the rules of our house; here we shared our joys and hid our sorrows. It had always been a hard discipline; now it seemed like a cruel one. Why couldn't we cry like other people?

"If you want me, you'll know where to find me. I guess." My mother was not amused. It was a feeble joke. An old complaint was that I was always disappearing, always running off to play just when I was needed.

There was a stillness in the dining room; the breathing of the soldiers seemed unduly heavy, my father's too effortful. When the telephone rang, we all started, even the soldiers. My father rose automatically, but he was pushed back roughly. A soldier picked up the phone. "Comrade Yurenko here. Yes. Yes. The mother and the father and the child. Yes. Nothing but two old people. Across the hall with Comrades Ivanov and Filipov. The rest are gone. No. I don't know. Empty apartments. Ten minutes is all that is needed." The phone went down with a bang.

Yurenko ordered my father to get dressed and get packed. I didn't know what to do or where to go. I settled on staying in the hall near my parents room. It seemed as if only a few seconds had passed before Yurenko wanted to know if they were ready.

"Certainly not," my mother said. "Not nearly ready, Comrade."

I admired my mother's bravery, but I was fearful that she had overdone it.

"You'll be ready all right. In exactly ten minutes we're leaving. Not a minute more."

Wisely, my mother didn't argue. She asked father to pack a wicker hamper with things like bed linen, a comforter, pillows, a pot or two, and some cutlery. To use where? I wondered. Somehow, before she left the bedroom she managed to whisper to Father that there was a little money hidden in her vanity.

When she came to my room carrying some of her clothes with her, I ran to her. "Mama, there are trucks in front of our house. I saw them."

She stood still for a second. "So . . . so there are trucks. Why haven't you put your things into a suitcase?"

"Mama—will we have to ride in the trucks? Like horses?"

"I don't know. What difference does it make? Esther . . . Esther, why didn't you do what you were told to do? Fetch a bag immediately."

I could not tell her that to close a suitcase on my belongings was more than I could bring myself to do, that I wanted to delay the finality of that snap as long as possible.

"Mama, where is everyone—Aunt Sonia and Uncle David?"

"Hush, Esther! They've gone. They left when they heard the soldiers. Esther, you simply cannot take these." She was holding the photo albums. "We need every bit of room for our clothes."

"Oh, please—please, I *need* them so badly. Truly I do. I'll put them in the bottom of the valise and I'll just take fewer clothes. I don't need the clothes nearly as much. I'd rather go barefoot. . . ."

My mother ignored me and started sorting the clothes, her hands moving with nervous speed. Close to hysterics, I begged and pleaded. She became impatient and finally very stern: the albums were not to go. Looking over her shoulder first, she whispered that someone was bound to question us about the people in these albums. Although I didn't understand the implications of this, something in her voice silenced me. Holding back my tears, I returned the albums to the shelf. Surreptitiously, I stroked them, saying my farewell.

Mother left and I stuffed the clothes into the bag, helter-skelter. My clothes consisted of some panties, vests, and slips, a nightgown, some socks and handkerchiefs, a navy-blue woolen school skirt, a white cotton blouse, a red and blue woolen sweater, and three cotton dresses. I had trouble stuffing a winter coat in and considered leaving it out. Fortunately, I didn't. That morning I was wearing a blue cotton dress, blue summer socks, and black oxfords.

The doorbell rang and I felt a great surge of hope: someone had come to save us! I flew into the dining room and looked into the hall. Yurenko was opening the door. My mother brushed past me and into the vestibule.

17

"Who is this man?" Yurenko asked.

Mother looked into her brother Liusik's white face and quietly said, "I don't know. I have never seen him before."

The soldier kicked the door shut. As Mother turned, I was about to ask her why she had said that when I remembered the albums and held my tongue.

Yurenko looked at his watch. "Your ten minutes is up. Get going."

I ran for my suitcase just as Father came out of the bedroom. Carrying two traveling cases, pigskin lined with morocco, he looked like a gentleman off on a holiday jaunt, one badly in need of a holiday. Mother followed him, carrying the wicker hamper.

When we walked out of our home into the bright sunshine, I realized that once again I had stepped out with my left foot forward. But this time I knew there was no right foot any place on earth to save us. Only one truck remained and it was waiting for us. It was filled with a blur of silent people. But on the sidewalk there was a murmur from dozens of curious onlookers. I couldn't understand what they were saying, nor did it matter.

Yurenko ordered us onto the truck. My father put his bags down and picked me up. I buried my face in his shoulder and he held me tighter. He set me down gently, next to a woman in a silk dress. The woman didn't move. Father helped Mother, who held her head high but whose cheeks were flaming throughout the awkward business of hoisting herself up. The suitcases and the hamper were next and then Father. Out of the blur of faces, I saw my grandfather's and grandmother's. There were no other members of our family on the truck.

I waved to my grandparents, but they made no sign that they had seen me. I lowered my eyelids. It was a good thing to do, it made it easier to face the crowd gawking at us from the street. It also made things move away, away from me, leaving me in a half-real daydream.

"Raya!" I heard my mother's name being called.

Grandmother Sara was standing alongside the truck. She looked at Mother, then covered her face with her hands.

The back door of the truck was bolted and the motor started. The truck began to rumble down Great Pogulanka Avenue, past our white house with its mahogany door—a curtain was blowing out the dining-room window—past our garden wall, down the avenue where I knew each house, each tree, each chipped stone on the sidewalk. Beneath my lowered lids I watched my world disappear forever.

I heard our names called hysterically. "Raya—Samuel —Esther—what is happening? Where are they taking you?" The voice faded, but I recognized my Aunt Sonia racing after the truck with her arms outstretched and her hair flying in the wind. "Oh, Sonia—" I called out to her and began to sob. My mother pressed my shoulders and softly urged me to stop weeping. I heard some others on the truck also whisper a soft "Shh . . . shh . . ." But I didn't stop; I thought it was time to weep.

19

Everyone else was quiet. Rumbling past the streets and the green parks and the market place of Vilna, in the bright sunlight they saw their fellow citizens going about their noonday business—marketing, pausing to gossip, sunning on a park bench. Witnessing the end of their world, this particular truckload of people was silent.

At the railroad station all was confusion: a huge mass of people was milling about; trucks, hundreds of them, were arriving from all directions, each one jammed with people. I searched for a familiar face but saw only the stricken faces of strangers. Why us? the question persisted. Why us?

A soldier with a much decorated chest came to our truck, a hero. He told us he would call our names, that we were to listen carefully to his orders. We listened. The list seemed interminable, but we were not overlooked. At last we heard: "Rudomin, Samuel, Raya, Esther. To the second train. Rudomin, Anna. To the second train. Rudomin, Solomon. To the first train."

My grandmother cried out. Never have I heard a more dreadful scream, not even in a nightmare. Torn out of this frail but proud woman, it came from unspeakable pain, but also from fury and sheer bewilderment. I looked at my grandfather. He was looking out over the confusion of people and trucks and soldiers, seeing nothing.

My grandmother was pleading with the soldier hero, my grandmother who had never in her life asked anyone for anything. "In God's name let me go with him. I want to go with my husband. I won't go without him. In God's name, I beg of you . . ." The medals jingled on the soldier's chest as he threw back his shoulders. "You'll do as you're told. No more out of you, old woman!"

In the midst of her anguish, my grandmother appeared to be astonished that anyone would speak to her that way. She put a handkerchief to her mouth and made no sound. My father tried to plead with the soldier, but his words were drowned as the soldier continued to bark instructions.

Finally, the last name had been called. The people who were to go to the first train made their brief farewells to their families and left the truck. My grandfather shuffled past us without a word.

"Sol-o-mon . . ."

Grandmother's wail slowly faded.

I wedged myself between my grandmother and my father. With one hand I stroked my grandmother's arm as she sobbed openly, and with the other hand I clung to my father, clung fiercely lest he too be taken away from me. Who knew whether this soldier might not change his mind?

When everyone who was to travel on the first train had been led away, my grandmother's sobs mingled with the quiet mass weeping on the truck.

The soldier ordered us to make a double line and we were marched off to the second train. I walked with Mother, while my father supported Grandmother. Each one of us lugged a suitcase—my mother, the hamper—and mine kept bumping against my leg or against Mother.

Ahead of us the cattle cars were waiting for their human cargo.

CHAPTER 2

The car stank of animals and the sun that was shining so benignly over Vilna had made a furnace of this place. Four small square holes high up in the corners of the car and the slivers of space between the filthy slatted walls were all that provided light and air. However, to be fair, cattle on their way to the slaughterhouse did not need a well-appointed car. Even in that twilight, one could see the scars on the floor made by those other beasts as they shuffled uneasily during their journey.

And now we shuffled, some forty of us, as we looked around us. Stood, huddled in the middle of the car, shuffling from foot to foot. No one talked.

There wasn't much to see. The car had been divided

in half, leaving a passageway between double rows of makeshift bunks. I was soon to discover that these wooden slabs were to be our beds, our tables, our chairs, our quarters.

No one knew what to do. My father took upon himself the job of leading this bewildered, shocked group of people. A gentle man, yet with a great capacity for making his presence felt and his orders obeyed, he now directed the older people to take the lower bunks and the young ones to climb to the uppers.

The crowd sighed. Victims of tyranny, they needed someone in authority, someone to tell them what to do. They began to select their bunks with a minimum of confusion; no one was in a mood to be fussy. Although Father had told me to climb a rickety ladder to an upper bunk, I stayed below to take a look at our traveling companions, our fellow capitalists. Possibly I imagined that by studying them I would uncover the secret of our own villainy, bring some sanity, however harsh, to this insanity. What I saw only added to my bewilderment; peering out from behind one of my braids, I saw nothing more villainous than peasants—women in shawls, men in cotton jackets and trousers that resembled riding breeches. I saw Polish peasants, not a rich capitalist among them; yanked from their land, they had toted their belongings in sacks, in shawls, in cardboard boxes. I saw reflected in their stricken faces our mutual shock.

Later we learned of reports that more than a million Poles had been deported as "class enemies."

The train jolted violently and began to move. I scrambled up to the upper bunk and crawled into the corner, near one of the holes that was to be our window. It was from this hole in a cattle car that I would see Vilna for the last time.

Vilna had been presented to me by my maternal great-grandmother Reisa as if it were a family heirloom. In a way it was. Vilna, which was the oldest seat of Jewish culture in eastern Europe, the Jerusalem of Europe, was also the place where many of my ancestors had distinguished themselves. Among them were rabbis, teachers, scholars, and leaders of social reform. Vilna was studded with the temples where they had preached, the schools they had organized, the libraries that housed their books.

Great-grandmother Reisa was the family historian, its chronicler. Vilna was her favorite topic. She was a rich old woman who looked rather like an old Spanish duchess, always in black and pearls, with a small black lace scarf on her graying hair. She was very religious and very eccentric. (In her large house, chickens to be slaughtered for supper had a special room of their own: "Where does it say that chickens must be kept in a chicken coop? *Where?*") And, to a child, she was a fascinating and a persuasive storyteller; always, as I walked the streets of Vilna, my ancestors walked beside me because of her. Later, when this eighty-five-year-old woman was told that the Nazis were on their way to take her from her home and ship her to some concentration camp or worse, she said, "Those Nazis will do no such thing. It is time for me to die and it is for me to say when and where. Not them. So I will die today, here, in my own house." And so she did: she lay down on her own bed, in her own black silk and pearls, in her own house, in her own beloved city, and picked the moment for dying herself. It was not suicide; by a supreme act of will, this old woman cheated the Nazis of her death.

I thought of Great-grandmother Reisa as I peered out through the hole of the cattle car.

I was exhausted and numb, but I was glued to that hole. Before long, I would get to hate the tormenting slowness of this train, but now it provided me with a ribbonlike souvenir of my childhood, the scenes around Vilna—a last glimpse of Castle Hill, the woods where we picnicked, the Wilja where the willows really seemed to weep today, past the small towns, the small farms, the summer homes. The summer homes? In a minute, ours would appear. I strained my eyes to the point where I almost couldn't see. There was the bend in the Wilja, there was the oak that was home free in tag, and there was the roof of our simple country house. I watched it disappear and then I buried my face in my hands.

The people in the car began to weep. And on the bunk below, I heard Grandmother begin to weep again and my father try to comfort her. My mother lay next to me like a figure on a sarcophagus, her hands under her head, her eyes tightly shut. Drained of color, her face—strong and beautiful—was more Spanish than ever, more like her grandmother Reisa's. I watched her and knew that she would not weep, not Mother. She did not and I did not. But the strain of not weeping, the sound of other people weeping, and the movement of the train put me to sleep. Sleeping would become a way of life; in the next weeks it would replace life.

I slept from the middle of that June day into the night, and I didn't wake up until early the next morning. When I awakened, I saw my mother sitting in the corner of the bunk staring at nothing. I asked her where we were and whether we had stopped anyplace during the night. She didn't know where we were and she couldn't remember what went on during the night. What difference did it make? But I needed reassurance and I climbed down to my father. He looked thoroughly exhausted; my grandmother was leaning against him as if she had spent the night in that position. Yesterday, in the midst of the terror, this frail little bird had left her house dressed as if she were off to lunch: she wore her customary silk, this time a delicate little print, and she had tilted over an eye one of her many tiny Garbo slouch hats, this one a soft black straw. She had not forgotten her gloves, white ones. During the night she had aged dreadfully. Her dress was crumpled and her gloves were streaked with dirt. She started to whimper weakly when she saw me, but she had no more tears in her. I didn't want to see her this way and I turned my head. This was the time of day, morning, when my stylish little grandmother would have been making her daily rounds in the family house. Wearing her hat and gloves, presumably she came to say good morning; more likely it was to see what the cooks were doing in the kitchens. As I said before, Grandmother Anna ruled rather majestically. But she had been gay and no one had minded.

Father assured me that we would try to find out where we were at the next stop, and he managed to smile at me. Father knew children; he knew they needed to know where they were. How else would they know where they were going? Even in a sealed cattle car, they needed this information. Even? Particularly in a sealed cattle car.

His smile helped; I turned my attention to familiar everyday needs. I needed to use a toilet. I also wanted to get out of my rumpled clothes, to wash my face and brush my teeth.

My mother might not know—or care—where we were, but she would surely know where the toilet was. I climbed back up to her. To my astonishment, she whispered that there was no toilet, that she would explain everything to me later. Later? I was horrified. Later could be too late.

"Hush! I'll comb your braids for you."

An inadequate substitute for a toilet, I thought.

After Mother had combed my hair, she said: "Perhaps we will get some soap and water later on. In the meantime, you may freshen yourself with some perfume."

She handed me the little crystal and silver perfume vial that she always carried in her pocketbook. I dabbed at my ears and temples and wrists as I had seen her do. How grown-up I would have felt to have been allowed to use perfume at home! In a second, mingling with the stench and heat of this cattle car was the famous and seductive scent of Guerlain's L'Heure Bleu. The irony of its name escaped me then.

I felt better and, although my need for a toilet was becoming more urgent, I realized that I was frightfully hungry too. I had not eaten in more than twenty-four hours and my stomach was rumbling noisily.

In the bunks opposite us, the peasants were eating.

They had brought huge slabs of cheese and boiled ham in their shawls.

"I'm hungry," I whispered.

My mother hushed me again and told me that we would get some food when the train stopped. Hearing this exchange, one of the women offered me a piece of ham and some cheese. My hand reached out, but to my distress my mother shook her head. "No, thank you," I was forced to say. "I'm not really hungry now." The woman seemed offended and I hastened to assure her that I appreciated her kindness—which I did indeed, much more than my mother's sensibility. The woman shrugged her shoulders and continued eating, smacking her lips and wiping them on her sleeve.

In what was to be the perpetual twilight of this car, I could see that all the peasants were eating. I looked to see if there were any other children, but the youngest among them were in their late teens. There was no more weeping, but no one was talking either. The only sounds were the smacking of lips, the creaking of the boards, the squealing of the wheels on the rails, and the chugging of the engine. Someone sneezed and never did a sneeze sound more human.

Although it was early morning, the car was hot and the air had become still more fetid, impossible as that seemed. Forty human beings—many of them not recently bathed—were not improving the animal smells. The heat and the stink would become worse and worse.

At last the train stopped. My heart beat violently. Were we there? Were we going to be let out of this inferno?

The bolt was pushed back and the door slid open. Fresh air. Forty pairs of lungs sucked it in. I started to move from the bunk; the objective was the open door. But a soldier hopped on and the door was closed behind him. He carried a pail of water and a ladle. He told us that this water was for drinking and for rinsing our faces. He pointed to a V-shaped opening opposite the door. That was where we were to wash and that opening was our toilet. Our toilet? No wonder my poor mother had resisted suffering this most animal-like indignity. The soldier told us that we were to get some food. He opened the door and jumped down onto a muddy platform. We had stopped at a tiny rural station.

Once again the door was closed and bolted.

So we were not to be released. Soon I would give up all expectation of this ever happening.

However, freedom was an abstraction; food was real and I became ravenous. When it arrived, it was nauseating. The soldier had returned with a rusty pail of soup; behind him another soldier carried wooden bowls and spoons. The steamy smell of cabbage soup was overpowering. I didn't dare refuse, but as soon as the soldier's back was turned, I put my bowl of soup down beside me, pinched my nose together, and turned to the window. Mother coaxed me to eat it; there would be no food for many hours, she warned, but nothing could make me eat that orange liquid where shriveled bits of tomato, carrots, and cabbage floated like refuse.

Now I concentrated on not vomiting. I lay down and turned my back. I heard my father ask the soldier where we were, but I no longer cared. Mother ate her soup and handed my uneaten portion to Father with the suggestion that either he or Grandmother should eat it. "We had better let her be," she said.

A wise decision, I thought, still fighting my nausea. And not an easy one for Mother to make. Mother, along with the rest of our family, took a child's refusal to eat hard.

Mother leaned over and whispered that I could now go to the toilet. Why did she bother to whisper that piece of public information? I was not yet used to whispering as a way of life. My father, she said, had managed to fashion a flimsy screen out of one of the precious sheets we had brought with us. The nausea had submerged all other sensations and I had quite forgotten about the toilet. But I went.

That adventure over, I went back to the bunk and fell asleep, holding my nose to close out the smell of cabbage.

And so we were on our journey—its route and its destination unknown. In the sinister twilight of that car, time too became an abstraction, but one the grownups clung to as if it were all that remained of sanity; they even squabbled over it. "Today must be the Sabbath. Isn't that so?" my grandmother would ask. My mother would disagree, which would upset my grandmother; my father would try to make peace. Everyone would remain uneasy. Was it or wasn't it the Sabbath? No one could tell for sure. Day was gray and night was black, but which day? which night?

Once a day, the soldiers brought the pail of soup and the pail of water; one wondered why they had gone to the trouble of adulterating water in order to call it soup, but even I began to accept it as something to eat some of the time. At other times, it was possible to buy fresh farmer cheese and black bread at a rural station. Only barely possible: the prices were outrageously high and some gymnastics were involved. Mother or Father would poke a head through the hole, shout down to the shabbily dressed peasants who were running up and down the platform with their produce, and begin to bargain noisily and with desperate haste. Once the price was set, they threw the money down, and then the job of handing the food up began. Usually, a child standing on a peasant's shoulders delivered the food to my parents' straining arms. Sometimes even a jug of milk made this wobbly trip. The money was never thrown down without the food's being sent up. The peasants of Poland and Russia may have been tough bargainers, but they were honest.

We slept; endlessly, the people in that cattle car slept. There was very little conversation—a word about the rain pouring through the four holes or a heat wave that would bring us close to suffocation, an occasional sardonic "good morning." We kept our fears to ourselves. What had become of Grandfather Solomon? Where was my beloved cousin Musik? My beloved Miss Rachel? At night sometimes when I looked through the hole, I saw the moon. When I was younger I had thought the moon was God. A rather too good child, I nevertheless used to make a list of my wrongdoings—an angry word to my mother, a fib to a playmate—and recite them to God when He appeared as the moon, and ask for His forgiveness. Now, when I saw the moon, I could only ask: What have I done wrong?

The soldiers refused to answer any questions: Where

are we? Where are we going? How much longer are we to be kept sealed up? We stopped asking them. But, from the accents of the peasants who sold us their produce, and the place names on the stations, Father was able to give us some notion of our general location. We were traveling through Byelorussia, the Ukraine, central Russia, chugging along about ten or twelve miles an hour, and sometimes staying for hours at a siding, perhaps to let another train go by, sometimes for no apparent reason at all unless it was to prolong our misery.

One day in the third or fourth week of this journey, Father, who had been looking through the hole, called to me to come quickly. I scrambled up beside him and he moved away so I could look out. We were approaching a ridge of mountains. To me, viewing it from a cattle car, the snow-covered peaks, the untouched pine forests were so painfully beautiful I almost wept. Father said, with wonder, that these must be the Urals, and that once we passed them we would be in Asia. Asia! I gasped. Asia? Well then, soon I would be seeing women in colorful costumes, bearded men in turbans, and the air would be heavy with the smell of spices. One still dreamed—in vain.

On the other side of the Urals, in Asia, the people at the stations were even shabbier than before, and the soup still smelled of cabbage, not spices. The scenery along the tracks was wilder and more desolate and our stops were less frequent. The daily ration of soup and water was served more irregularly, and it became more difficult and much more expensive to buy bread and milk. On the rare occasions when food was offered at a station, I watched Mother dole out her money with an anxiety that made me pretend I wasn't hungry. I could see that the money was already running out.

I had developed a fever—very likely I wasn't the only one who had—and between that, the heat, the stench, and the lice, my body itched incessantly. My braids had become dirty and lifeless. Going to the toilet and changing one's clothes—rotating the few unlaundered clothes one had—were major undertakings. The thought of a bath, a hair wash, and fresh clothes became an obsession.

When I wasn't sleeping feverishly, I would spend the days looking disconsolately through the hole and praying for this train to stop. Who cared what was at the end of this journey? Just let it end. I felt perpetually hungry, and with the hunger there was chronic fatigue. When the train stops moving and we get out, I'll feel much better, I would assure myself.

One day, after we had stopped at a town where the unpainted wooden station was a little larger, where the gingerbread under the eaves was more elaborate, where the water tower was more imposing, the soldier who usually brought us our food in total silence could not restrain himself: he whispered to Father that the Germans had invaded Russia on a huge front. Now Russia was at war too, along with the British! What, Mother wanted to know, did this mean for us, the captives of the Russians? My father shrugged: who knew?

The soldier went back to his silent ways and we heard no more about the war.

We had been traveling six weeks by my father's count when the train stopped. We were used to long waits and no one thought anything of it. The train would move again; it always had. I heard some commotion, and for some reason I thought that perhaps we had developed engine trouble, which would only prolong the journey.

I sat up to look out and, to my amazement, I saw that at this little railroad station there was a crowd milling around the train's first cars. Our end was deserted, except for a few soldiers here and there.

Then I saw the doors of the cars being opened, one by one, and people leaping out of them. I still couldn't believe that we, in this car, would be released. I couldn't believe it. But at last our door was opened too.

No soup and water this time. Instead, a soldier read from a document that sounded very much like the one I had heard—was it centuries ago?—in Vilna.

We had reached our destination. We were now in Rubtsovsk in the Altai Territory of the Russian Soviet Federated Socialist Republic of the great and mighty Soviet Union.

There were no cheers in that car. Forty people gathered their belongings together, silently, in a near frenzy, as if there were some danger that the door would close again and leave them behind in that car.

CHAPTER 3

The train had stopped moving, but not the earth: the muddy platform rocked under my feet. I had expected to be elated; instead, I was numb. Like a little old woman—which, in some ways, I had become—I ached from head to toe and, crouching, as if it were a position my body had grown into, I sat down on my suitcase.

After the weeks of twilight, daylight was too much— too strong, too strange.

Around me, I felt more than I saw the presence of hundreds of people, a lumpish mass, all numb like me.

Suddenly, there was a voice shouting at us. It must

have come from a primitive loud-speaker and I strained to catch the indistinct words: we were to pick up our bundles; we were to march four abreast behind the soldiers into the village.

What village? Where was it?

I began to take notice. For weeks, the question had been where were we going? Now we were there. But where was there? This rural station was just like all the others we had passed on this side of the Urals—a small wooden building on a muddy platform, gingerbread carved under all the eaves.

And beyond. Beyond was eternity. Flat, desolate, treeless world without end.

"Tata!"

"Lalinka."

My father held my hand for a second and then we fell into place, the four of us in one row.

Hundreds of us trudged down a narrow, dusty road toward a barely visible cluster of buildings. Presumably, way off there on the horizon was the village. Without a single tree to stop it, the July sun was like a torch on our heads. Surely every last one of us must have dreamed of the moment when we would once again breathe some fresh air. But this air, for all its vastness, was more hot than fresh.

When the first old woman fainted, there was a murmur of fear from the marching people. Had the woman fainted or had she dropped dead? She had fainted and, whether she wished it or not, she was revived and continued to march. I looked apprehensively at Grandmother: her silk dress was stained with sweat, but the ridiculous little hat on her dirty gray hair was like a tattered banner, our personal standard, the symbol that we still stood together as a family. This tiny figure would survive this march: I willed her to do so. She did—without any help from me, having quite enough will of her own. But at least a dozen old women, and old men too, dropped onto the road, sending up little clouds of dust as they did so.

Trudging this road that was like a hairline cut into a barren, grayish field of incredible size, I felt myself to be too little for anything so enormous. Once in a while, we would see a very small, single-roomed hut at the side of the road. These huts were square and made of mud and cow dung, as I was to learn from personal experience. Sometimes a shabbily dressed, barefoot woman of unknown age would stare at us curiously; sometimes she would be joined by rather solemn-faced children; but neither the women nor the children ever raised a hand in greeting.

After we had marched about a mile in the broiling sun, the huts were closer together, and now we could see one or two log cabins with whitewashed stoops.

In 1941, Rubtsovsk was nothing more than a village, all gazetteers to the contrary. That this speck in the middle of nowhere became a town of some industrial importance within some twenty years is a tribute to the people who made it possible; certainly not least among them were the hundreds who came there on that July day. They would make their contribution, indeed they would.

My first glimpse of Rubtsovsk was of a frontier village built around a large open square in straight lines, as if the muddy paths were laid out for ticktacktoe. Immediately surrounding the square were the market stalls, open wooden sheds. These were empty that day. Once again the loud-speaker crackled with authority; this time we were ordered to arrange ourselves in family groups in the square and await further instructions. Since families had clung to each other, this was done with dispatch.

The square was even hotter than the road, the sun being reflected from its cobblestones of all sizes and shapes. I stepped closer to my mother.

"Mama," I whispered, "doesn't this remind you of the market in *Uncle Tom's Cabin?*"

She wiped the sweat from her face and tried to smile but couldn't. "Perhaps it does . . . perhaps . . ."

My father did manage a smile, a rueful one. "Don't worry, lalinka, no one is going to buy us. Fortunately, they are short of ready cash. . . ."

Lalinka. I sighed. I was still Tata's little darling; the square seemed less horrid and now I needed to go to the toilet. Poor Mama. In the midst of a cataclysm, she also had to contend repeatedly with a child's bladder—or thirst; I was also thirsty. No, I couldn't look for a bathroom and water in the market stalls.

"But I've got to go . . ."

"You've got to *wait*. I can't lose sight of you. Do you want to get lost?"

To take my mind off toilets—no easy task—I looked at the people around us. Peasants, city people like us, women, men, teen-agers, and children, a rumpled, dirty, haggard company well acquainted in misery. And unreal. The soldiers standing guard around the square were not real either. We were so quiet, so motionless, that standing there in that strange square, in that vastness, our eyes squinting in the cruel sun, we were like a crowd waiting for a gun to go off. Every once in a while a head would barely nod as eyes met in guarded recognition—was it safe to know each other from the past?—and the motion seemed excessive in the stillness.

At last there was some movement at one side of the square. The soldiers made way for a group of men, about twenty of them, who marched into the square and separated as they moved into the crowd.

I watched the one who was coming toward us, and I gripped my father's hand tighter. He was a mean-looking man, tall and swarthy, with a pock-marked face full of hate.

"You!" He pointed a long-nailed dirty finger at Father. "What do you do? What's your work?"

"I'm an electrical engineer by training."

The man looked as if that was as boring a piece of information as he had ever heard. He asked Mother the same question and when she answered that she had once taught arts and crafts, but that now she was a housewife, he made a derisive noise, as if to say, What are we burdened with this time, a bunch of riffraff?

"And what can you do?" He leered at me as if I were his last hope.

"Why, she's nothing but a child," Mother said in panic. "A child. She goes to school."

Finished with his fun, he introduced himself as Popravka and told us that he was from the gypsum mine twelve kilometers outside the village. Before he walked away, he warned us not to dare move until he came back. As if we would in this barren land where there was literally no place to hide.

When Popravka returned, he announced that most of us were going to the gypsum mine with him, but that some would go to the collective farm. Farm? I had a picture of a lovely bucolic life with cows and chickens and hay rides. The mine sounded dreadful; one would be imprisoned in the bowels of the earth and one would die.

"What's gypsum, Tata?" I whispered.

But he was listening intently to Popravka as he ticked people off for mine or farm. Farm, farm, farm, I prayed silently; to play safe, I also kept my fingers crossed.

"Mine!" Popravka pointed at Father, Mother, and me. "Farm!" He pointed to Grandmother.

My heart sank. Mine or farm, what did it matter? What mattered was that we be allowed to stay together; all we had in the whole world was each other.

Grandmother began to plead again as she had at the railroad station in Vilna. This time our prayers were heard.

She was allowed to go with us, but she was warned that the work would be hard and that she would be expected to do her share. She drew herself up to her full four feet eleven inches, and assured him that she had the strength of a dozen young women. She was quietly convincing.

However, there were others who were not as lucky as we. All around us were families begging to stay together. When this was denied, there would be the all too familiar wail; when the request was granted, an embrace.

Popravka told us to pick up our suitcases, which, like us, were covered with dust, and to follow him. This was easier said than done; we were burdened with bags and hampers and bundles, and racing after one's jailer does not come naturally. At the edge of the square, we came upon dozens and dozens of trucks, open trucks, some already filled with people. When we reached ours, my mother became excited: "Look who is here," she whispered. "Look! Mrs. Marshak!"

This time, Mother jumped up onto the truck by herself, and dropping her guard, openly embraced this friend from Vilna. Mrs. Marshak, a woman noted for being austere, welcomed the embrace with tears of joy. It soon became clear that she had made the six-week journey in the cattle car without friend or family, except for Boris, her five-year-old boy. Boris, who had lost much of his chubbiness on the journey, had his almond-shaped green eyes fixed on my father. When Father held out his hand, he became, with that gesture, Boris's father, hero, friend, and mentor.

Popravka sat down beside the driver and we started down the road, raising great clouds of dust. Once, through the dust, I saw a patch of flowers next to a hut. I remembered what Grandfather Solomon had said about people who loved flowers, and I thought anyone who loved flowers enough to make them grow here must have more than a little good in him.

The flatness of this land was awesome. There wasn't a hill in sight; it was an enormous, unrippled sea of parched and lifeless grass.

"Tata, why is the earth so flat here?"

"These must be steppes, Esther."

"Steppes? But steppes are in Siberia."

"This is Siberia," he said quietly.

If I had been told that I had been transported to the moon, I could not have been more stunned.

"Siberia?" My voice trembled. "But Siberia is full of snow."

"It will be," my father said.

Siberia! Siberia was the end of the world, a point of no return. Siberia was for criminals and political enemies, where the punishment was unbelievably cruel, and where people died like flies. Summer or no summer —and who had ever talked about hot Siberia?—Siberia was the tundra and mountainous drifts of snow. Siberia was *wolves*.

I had been careless. I had neglected to pray to God to save us from a gypsum mine in Siberia.

CHAPTER 4

Gypsum, it turned out, was a grayish-white powder dug out of a desolate land by people in despair. It was mined to make plaster casts for wounded soldiers.

The site of this mine was bleak, so bleak that it made the village of Rubtsovsk attractive by comparison. Adjacent to the gouged earth, twelve mud huts stood in a straight line. They were flanked by a large wooden building and a small wooden building; no gingerbread here. And all around it was the unbroken, treeless steppe of Siberia, scorched by a blazing sun, without so much as a cloud to protect it. As far as the eye could see, there was no visible connection to the rest of the world.

Four truckloads of people—about one hundred and fifty—had been assigned to this mine, and now we were sent to the larger of the two wooden buildings. Once inside, it was obvious that this building was a school that had been stripped of everything but its blackboards and four huge portraits of Lenin, Stalin, Marx, and Engels. Six rooms opened off a main corridor and the twenty-six of us who had traveled on the same bus filed into one of them.

Popravka invited us to make ourselves at home. Our host was the only one who laughed—raucously—at his gallows humor. The room was completely bare of furniture—no chairs, no table, and most certainly no beds.

Children persist in asking questions. "Where are we going to sleep, Tata? On the floor?"

Even Father lost his patience. "No, Esther," he said sharply, "we will sleep on the ceiling like flies."

"It's already occupied by them, so there won't be any room for us," I retorted crossly. Indeed, the place was swarming with flies.

"Go, Esther, go get a drink of water, go to the bathroom . . . go. . . ."

Tata, as usual, was an incurable optimist.

I found Popravka in the corridor. "Excuse me, Mr. Popravka . . ."

"*Comrade* Popravka," he shrieked. "Comrade, always comrade, from now on—do you understand?"

"Yes, Comrade," I said meekly. "Please, Comrade Popravka, where can I get a drink of water, Comrade, and where is the bathroom, please, Comrade?"

"Not so many comrades," he shrieked even louder. "One or two is enough. And the bathroom is an outhouse"—which, he implied, throwing back his shoulders, was another triumph over capitalism.

I did not know what an outhouse was, but I was afraid to ask this comrade. In due course, I found out.

We were one of four lucky groups: Father had found us living quarters in a corner of the room. In an utterly bare room, two walls to lean against, a corner to curl up into, were luxury. Mrs. Marshak and Boris were across the room from us, and it was a comfort to see their familiar faces. However, the strangers around us were not quite so strange as the ones in the cattle car; except for one or two peasants, for the most part these were the faces from my past—the shopkeepers and middle-class professionals of Vilna. The only genuine capitalist, from a Soviet point of view, was my father, who, along with his family, had owned a very large business. It seemed to please everyone that Father, who had helped with their baggage, was a well-known citizen of Vilna.

Once again there was no one my own age here.

Settled on the floor, we all used our belongings as back rests, seats, pillows. And we waited. Even I, a child, had begun to feel oppressed. One had not the freedom to fetch so much as a glass of water by oneself. One waited to have water doled out. One waited. The flies buzzing around in the heat were free. I hated them, not for being flies, but for being free.

Finally, the door opened. A boy appeared carrying a pail of water and one tin cup. He had a sunburned face and he was smiling. He was *friendly*. I could have hugged him.

"Anyone want a drink?" he asked.

The boy was nearly mobbed.

He dipped the cup into the pail and held it out. Dozens of hands reached for it. "Wait a minute," he said, looking around. A boy with water also had authority. Then he came toward us and handed the cup to Grandmother, who took a sip. Refreshed by the water, but even more so by the boy's deference, Grandmother lifted her head and became the matriarch—for this moment at least. "See that everyone has water," she said. The boy took it for granted that an old woman could issue orders; he nodded his head. Encouraged, Mother put in her two cents, the first time in weeks. "Let the old people have first turn, then the children, and what's left over we will drink." This became the procedure, with Grandmother deciding who was old and who was not. Waiting my turn, my thirst had become so great that I nearly challenged Grandmother: she was picking some awfully young old people, it seemed to me. Would there be one drop of water left for me? No one, including of all people my antiseptic mother, appeared to mind drinking out of one cup. When my turn came, I took such a big sip that I was forced to blow my cheeks out to hold the water until I could swallow it in tiny, tiny gulps to make it last. Now it was camels I envied.

The pail of water was finished and I was impressed with us as a group. There had been no fights, no one had pulled a knife, no one had done any of the things I had seen thirsty people do in the movies.

Popravka came in and once again told us not to move, that we would be called to a meeting. Popravka's concern that he would lose one of his prisoners bordered on the insane. We did not move; we waited. The old people dozed; some people stretched out and rested their heads on their clasped hands and stared into space. I put my head in my father's lap and he twisted one of my braids around my nose. Mother, who normally would have objected that the dirty hair would make me sneeze, this time only looked sad.

Had I changed as much as Mama, Tata, and Grandmother had? They looked so old, so bedraggled, so dirty. I held up my hand. It was black with grime. My hair smelled horrid around my nose and I pushed it away.

Popravka came back and ordered us to march out and line up in front of the schoolhouse. We did so and again we waited. Were we now to be sent to the mine? Would we never again see the sun, which was hotter than before and boiling us alive?

Presently, a man came out of the smaller building and stood in front of us. Popravka introduced him as Comrade Alexander Ivanovich Makrinin, director of the gypsum mine. Comrade Makrinin stood in front of us, for what seemed like ages, scanning the rows and rows of faces before him; then he looked down at the ground. My heart was beating fast and I imagined I could hear all the other hearts beating too.

"Welcome . . . welcome to the mine," he said at last.

The crowd stirred. Was this more of Popravka's brand of malicious humor? But no, Makrinin had spoken gently, kindly; he meant to ease our pain. He kept on speaking gently in Russian. Even I, who knew little Russian, could tell it was more cultivated than Popravka's, and it sounded like music after the harsh, demeaning bark of the soldiers and of Popravka. For the first time in weeks, someone was addressing us as if we were human beings. Not one person among the hundred and fifty who stood there wished to be welcomed to this mine, but a gentle voice in a jailer made us feel less imprisoned.

Makrinin, a stocky man with a round, flat face, continued to speak gently and kindly, without anger or meanness, rather with regret that we were all in this dreadful business together. He told us to arrange ourselves in family groups; he would then come to us and assign us to our tasks, which would start in the morning. He assured us that if we needed assistance we were to go directly to his office in the small building. Also, it was there that we would be given our rations of bread; he hesitated before he added the words ". . . and other provisions." Tonight there would be pails of soup in each room; tomorrow there would be bread.

When he came to our family, Makrinin greeted my father with a courteous "*Zdrastvuytie,*" hello in Russian. "I understand that you are an electrical engineer by profession. Here we have nothing like that for you to do. However . . . we are in need of someone to drive a horse and cart."

My father shrugged. "I have ridden horses, but I have never driven one, nor harnessed one. I will do my best."

"Yes, that is a good idea." He turned to my mother. "You . . . you will work with a group of women and you will be in charge of them—"

"What kind of work?"

"Dynamiting the mines."

"Dynamiting?" Mother's overheated face went white. Father broke in. "Oh—please—why can't I do this?

My wife could drive the buggy, that she could do I'm sure——"

Makrinin flushed. "The orders are for the men to drive carts and work in the mine. The women will dynamite, the children will work in the fields, and the old people will shovel the gypsum." He was embarrassed. "Those are my orders," he said softly. "Now you may return to the school and rest if you wish." He turned away from us and went to the next group as quickly as he could.

We walked back to the room silently. Huddled together in our corner, Father finally exploded: "Insanity! Insanity! Peasants are capitalists. Engineers drive horses. Women dynamite. What next? What next?"

"Samuel! For God's sake, don't talk so loud. Someone will hear you. Here the walls have ears. Remember that." She had been whispering of course, but now she whispered directly into my ear: "Remember that, Esther." Then, "It isn't as bad as it could have been. At least we aren't in a concentration camp——"

"What did you say?" Grandmother asked. "What did you say about a concentration camp?"

"I said we should be thankful we're not in one——"

"Is Solomon in one? Are you keeping something from me?"

My father scowled at Mother. "No, no." He put his arm around his mother. "Father is most certainly in an-another place like this—most certainly——"

"Some blessing!" Grandmother said sarcastically. "But if that is so, why aren't we all here together? Why?"

"Why? Because it is as I just said. Everything is insane, senseless——" Mother pointed frantically to the walls, and he dropped his voice until it was barely audible. "The right hand doesn't know what the left is doing."

Grandmother stretched out on the wooden floor and shielded her eyes with her arm. I saw her lips working: Solomon, Solomon . . .

In our family, as in most European families of my childhood, old people were treated with special reverence. Now to see old men and old women sprawled on the bare floor without a tiny shred of comfort for their old bones seemed, particularly to a child, like a shocking breach of etiquette.

That night the room was almost as hot as the cattle car. There was no light and, in the darkness, it seemed even more crowded, perhaps because of the vastness outside. Flies buzzed incessantly and, to make matters worse, they had been joined by midges. Twenty-six people tried to sleep, and their bodies, turning and twisting on the floor, made the boards creak and groan. Occasionally, someone who had fallen asleep would cry out in a nightmare, and each time this happened Boris howled with fright. His fear was a boon to me, making me feel quite grown-up by comparison and less afraid.

At last the moon came up. I was afraid to go to a window to see it, but a moonbeam lit up some of the prone bodies. In this world, one did the best one could with what one had. I reverted to the time when I was younger and I spoke to the shaft of moonlight. I thanked God for making me a little girl who would not have to use dynamite in a mine or shovel gypsum. I thanked God for allowing me to work in a field. I thought it was very saintly of me to be so thankful in this terrible place and I fell asleep.

At about three o'clock in the morning, I heard a knock at the window near us. Father heard it too and sat up, remaining motionless. There was another knock and then, appearing at the window—and disappearing almost at once—was the face of a young girl. Father tiptoed to the window and leaned out. Two young girls from the village had stolen a watermelon and cut it up to give to the Polish slave laborers. They handed the slices up to Father and silently, silently, these were passed from person to person. The girls fled before Father could say thank you properly.

Those of us who were lucky enough to have had a slice of that watermelon that night—like me—must count it the most delectable food ever eaten anyplace by anyone.

"Perhaps . . . perhaps . . . it will not be so terrible here after all," Father whispered before he went back to sleep.

The truth is that he was both right and wrong, very wrong.

The next morning a whistle blew. At six o'clock that morning it was like a whip that lashed everyone to his feet. Since no one had undressed that first night, toilets consisted of straightening a skirt, pulling a trouser belt, smoothing a dirty head of hair. Later, those who had brought sheets or comforters would use them as dressing rooms, squirming beneath them; those less fortunate would use coats—or the outhouse.

51

Popravka stamped into the room. In the early-morning light, he looked more hateful than ever, as if he had been brewing venom in his sleep.

"Women dynamiters—right. Men miners—left. Men truckers—forward. Children and old women—back of me."

In my view, we were all children, every last one of us. Who ever ordered grownups around this way? old grownups? civilian grownups?

We did as we were told: there were no rebels among us, not then, not later. Outside, the steppe was vast and silent—not even a bird was overhead that morning— and it became Popravka's accomplice in reducing us to insects.

"When the whistle blows again," Popravka informed us, "some hours from now, go to the director's office. You will get bread there."

I watched Mother go off to dynamite, Father to drive a cart, and Grandmother to shovel. There was not so much as a second to say good-by. Until now, we had been together day and night for six weeks, been inseparable. Now suddenly I was alone. And desolate. I had been reared in the midst of a clan, I had had Miss Rachel as my constant companion. Under the best of circumstances, I was not a child who made friends easily. I felt dismembered.

Left behind, standing forlornly, we were about a dozen children—once again none of them my age— each more bedraggled and dirtier than the next. One little girl, still somewhat plump after six weeks of near starvation, began to howl; an older girl, obviously her sister, tried to comfort her without success. Just then the boy who had smiled when he brought us our water joined us. He looked over his shoulder before going up to the little girl. Pulling his lower lids down and poking his nose up, he made a pig face for her; he also grunted. It worked; she smiled through her tears, and we all felt better.

He led us to the potato patch and on the way he shed the role of happy-go-lucky, smiling young boy and became a serious and stern young man as he lectured us: We were to do our work well. No! That would not be good enough, we were to do our work to perfection. If we did not weed properly, there would be no potatoes next winter; if there were no potatoes, we would all starve. Did any among us enjoy starving? he inquired severely. "No!" we cried out from the bottom of our empty bellies.

I knew that I would do well, thanks to Grandfather Solomon; he had taught all of us children to be good gardeners. "You must get your hands into the earth," he would tell us. But even covered with soil up to his elbows, he himself still managed to look immaculate in his gardening clothes, his elegant little beard snow white in the sunlight. The squeamish among us soon learned to keep our distaste for worms to ourselves; while Grandfather did not absolutely insist that we *love* worms, he made it quite clear that he would not tolerate anything less than coexistence. But weeds he would not tolerate. "So, my grandchildren, what is it to be? a tangle or a garden?" "A tangle, a tangle, a beautiful tangle," my cousin Salik would answer as he leaned against a tree, feigning exhaustion. Salik was my grandfather's favorite, a marvelously merry and wild boy whom we all adored. Salik . . . I almost called his name aloud, the way Grandmother called to Grandfather. For a second, I had a fantasy that standing there close to the top of the world, with nothing to stop the sound, I could call out to my cousins, one by one, and to Miss Rachel, and that wherever they were they would hear me.

But I was a practical child; I followed the others to the potato patch. One look at it convinced me that we would indeed starve that winter. Instead of having the green leaves and the pretty white flowers of a healthy, bountiful potato crop, these plants were brown and parched. My stomach contracted with a hunger pain. What was needed was a magic wand in order to harvest a crop here. Didn't they know that?

A barefoot woman wearing a babushka came toward us and clapped her hands for attention. "Comrade children!" Whether this salutation was meant to be only proper or sarcastic or humorous, it sounded funny. Neither then nor subsequently did she introduce herself, but very few people we were to meet did; 1941 was not the time and Siberia was not the place for introductions. For the most part, the native Siberians were the descendants of the early exiles—the criminals (crime under the tsars having constituted anything from neglecting to remove one's cap in the presence of one's superior to murdering him), the political prisoners, the escaped serfs, and the self-exiled who were adventurers or Cossacks in search of trade. Whoever and whatever their ancestors were, they had one thing in common, these native *Siberyaki*—their pride in being the descendants of early settlers. After the Revolution, in the twenties and thirties, came another great wave of exiles, the kulaks. And whenever my parents couldn't decide who was who in Siberia, they would invariably guess "kulak." Whether they were right or wrong, we never knew; in fact, our life was so circumscribed that most of the people around us were only figures on a lantern slide seen without narration.

All this did not unfold itself that morning. That morning potatoes took precedence over people, a condition that was to endure in Siberia.

The woman repeated the warning that if we did not do our work properly we would starve the coming winter. She plucked a thin blade of grass from the ground and held it up. "Weed! No good! Out!" She pointed to a straggly little potato vine. "Potato. Very good. Belongs in. In! Do not pull potato with weed. Pull nicely. Pull with care. Pull to *eat* next winter."

I knelt on the ground and began to weed with the peculiar knowledge that for once my life really did depend upon the quality of my performance.

Suddenly, to my horror, I saw that the boy ahead of me had pulled out some potato leaves.

"Hey you—" I whispered frantically. "Psst!"

"What *is* it?"

I told him. I crawled up to him. I showed him once again what a weed was. "For God's sake, be careful, you——"

"All right, all right—you *farmer*, you!"

I promised not to tell on him if he promised to be more careful. He called me a pest, but yes, he could weed as well as any *girl* could.

We worked on and on. The sun got hotter and hotter. And we were not children used to working the land. However, I enjoyed it. It was the best morning I had had in weeks.

The whistle blew and we straightened up and waited. The woman told us to go back to the schoolhouse and join our families there.

We didn't run back—none of us felt free enough to do that—but we went as swiftly as possible. The grownups, our mothers and fathers, came from the mine, every one of them sweating heavily and even more disheveled and distracted than they had been before. My mother's hair was tumbling down and she was limping, and my father looked as if he had suffered sunstroke. Grandmother seemed close to collapse; her eyes sunken into her exhausted face were more bewildered than wounded. Whatever is everyone thinking of? they seemed to say.

Another whistle blew and Popravka told us to line up at Makrinin's office. There we were each given three hundred grams of bread, which was to be our standard daily ration, and a small piece of brinza, the sheep cheese which was kept in barrels of salt water. The door to the storeroom was open and I sidled toward it, hoping that I would see something in it besides bread and brinza. What I saw were bags of flour and a very large supply of huge bottles filled with a clear fluid. Creeping still closer, I saw that the bottles were labeled cologne. Cologne? Were we—this hungry, dirty crowd, crawling with lice—to be doused with cologne in lieu of a bath? How very refined, I thought.

Popravka ordered us to eat quickly—How long did he think it would take to swallow one piece of bread? my father inquired under his breath—and said that when the whistle blew again we were to return to work. We sat on the floor in our places in the schoolhouse. We cut our bread, which weighed more, for being underdone, and our cheese in half and ate it; the other half we wrapped in handkerchiefs, scarves, paper if anyone had any, whatever was at hand, and put away for supper. Brinza would now be added to the smells of the room. At what point, I wondered, would they dole out the cologne? And, being a stickler for these matters, I even wondered whether its scent would be pleasing.

The whistle blew before we even had had a chance to talk to each other. As we marched out, my father asked anxiously: "Are you all right, lalinka?"

"Of course I am and besides I'm having fun too," I replied.

Father looked at me as if he thought that things were bad enough without having me go crazy too.

The afternoon would have been more fun if it had ended about an hour after lunch. But it didn't. The rows became longer and longer as the afternoon dragged on. And the heat became more intense. I tried to push it away as hard as I could, but all I could think of was the river in front of our summer house and Musik and me racing to the float. Or Mama, who was a marvelous swimmer, teaching me to kick 1-2-3, kick 1-2-3, kick 1-2-3. "Keep your knees straight, Esther." If one kept one's knees straight, one would grow up to be a great swimmer and beautiful like Mama.

The water of the river was cool and clear and one could see the silvery minnows scurrying away as Musik swam underneath like a beautiful silvery fish himself.

I tried not to think of the river.

"A potato! You pulled a potato!" the woman shrieked at someone. The woman too was getting tired and cranky under the broiling sun. "Dunce! We will starve! Dunce, do you want us all to starve?"

I bent my head closer to the vines; I didn't want to see *the* dunce. But as a member of collective dunce, I too called out, "No, no." We were not humanitarians; we were just hungry children who didn't want to starve, and I think it likely that collectively we had it in us to stone the next child who pulled a potato.

Even in Siberia things came to an end; at last the whistle blew.

At the close of the day's work, the exhausted people in our room had made one gain: they had achieved a reserved fellowship, a subtle something that said, "Well, here we are in a gypsum mine in Siberia, it is a fact that we are in it together, and together we have survived. They began to talk to each other—always guarded, in whispers, but to talk.

The women told how they had drilled holes, the jackhammers shaking the life out of them, blistering their hands. Mother, who had worked in sandals, winced when she took them off; her feet were a blistered mess. Dropping her voice, so that only we could hear, she said that she wished the women she supervised weren't so hysterical because the next day they were going to use dynamite. My mother thought it highly likely that they would blow themselves up.

"And what did you do, Tata?" I asked quickly.

"I was hoping someone would ask me that question." His face was gaunt and streaked with gypsum, his once blond hair was an ugly brown and was plastered to his head with sweat and dirt, but his eyes were merry. "You see before you a great wagoner, a jehu." He bowed. "It was my job to harness the horse to the wagon, load it with gypsum, and drive it to a truck. So, I harnessed the horse to the wagon, yes? A simple matter, correct? Many fools have done it, why not this one? However, this being my first time and me being a conscientious man, it took me longer—maybe ten times as long as another fool. I worked hard, I did everything that was to be done. The horse, I might say, was very co-operative. A sympathetic animal, he stood absolutely still. At last it was done—he was harnessed. And we were both pleased, very pleased. Siberia or no Siberia, there is satisfaction in a job well done. Next, I heaved the gypsum onto the wagon. Gypsum, as we have all learned today, weighs more than a feather, but it was finally on the wagon, each and every ton of it." Father, who loved to tell stories, even in a voice just above a whisper, grunted and placed his hand on the small of his back. The other people, who had crowded close to listen, inadvertently grunted too. "I jumped up," he went on, "took the reins in my hand and said, 'Giddyup.' The horse, being also an obedient horse, obeyed the command and trotted off. There was only one thing wrong, a detail. He left me behind. Left me sitting there all by myself, while he trotted off. That, my friends, is a Siberian horse for you—treacherous."

The laughter that followed was cracked from disuse, Siberian laughter. But it was laughter. Much that we would think funny in the days to come would scarcely have caused the shadow of a smile at home in Vilna but we needed to laugh as much as we needed bread.

"And how did your day go, Mother?" Father asked Grandmother.

"How was it supposed to go? I shoveled that stuff. All day long I shoveled it."

She began to riffle through her belongings, obviously searching for something vital.

"I have the valerian," Mother said. Mother had packed valerian and powders for her migraine headaches; no other drugs. Valerian was used in our family for dizziness, faintness, stomach ache, and hurt feelings.

"Who needs valerian?" Grandmother muttered. Then she sighed; she found what she wanted. It was her little leather manicure kit. Sitting on the floor of a barren schoolroom in Siberia, covered with gypsum dust from head to toe, my tiny grandmother proceeded to push back her cuticle. Every night before she lay down to sleep she would continue to do this. She had exceptionally beautiful hands.

That night, as I lay on the floor, rows and rows of potato plants floated past my closed eyes. Baked potatoes. Stuffed potatoes. Mashed potatoes. Creamed potatoes. Fried potatoes. I ran out of ways to prepare potatoes and I turned over on my stomach and made a pillow of my arms. I must have fallen asleep, because the whistle woke me.

The next morning, just as I was about to pull another weed, I heard the blast, felt the earth tremble under me. All of us children froze, and then stared toward the mine; our mamas and our papas were in that mine.

"Comrade children, get on with your work. You'll get used to dynamiting."

Not that morning. Every time there was a blast, I sickened with terror. When it was time for lunch and I saw my parents and grandmother with my own eyes, saw that they had survived, I gave each one of them a big hug—much to their embarrassment: we were not a demonstrative family. Later, I would occasionally watch my mother work with the jack hammer, but the woman whose guts seemed about to be shaken out of her, whose face was contorted to ugliness, would seem a stranger.

We got used to many things: the heat, the vermin, the scarcity of food, the hard work.

Other things. Like men who reeked of cologne and staggered as they walked. The first time I sidestepped one of these native Siberian men, I reported it to Mother, complete with a demonstration, but she was as baffled as I was. Were these men using cologne because they were dizzy or had they become dizzy from applying too much of it? Of course they had drunk it. It seemed that in that mine, where vodka was in short supply or nonexistent, any alcohol would do, including that found in highly scented cologne.

My education was beginning. I was to learn many things in Siberia. And one of them was how *not* to wash one's hair. One day when my dirty hair and the itching of my scalp had become unbearable, I asked Mother if I could wash my hair during the lunch period. She said that if I was under the impression that I could get my hair clean without soap, I had her permission to dump some water on my head. So, instead of lunch that day, I raced to the pump at the side of the schoolhouse, where we more or less sponged ourselves, with or without privacy—usually without. Today, since everyone was inside eating lunch—a grandiose word for a piece of bread—I had privacy. I filled a pail with water and thought it was silly of my mother to have forgotten that we had learned to wash our hands with clay the way the Siberian women did. The clay not only cleaned one's hands, but left them smooth and slightly yellowish. Since I had always longed to be blond like my father, nothing would have pleased me more than if my brown hair was yellowed up a bit. I clawed the clay out of the ground and rubbed it into my scalp and hair generously. The result was a head baked in a crust. Not only did the clay resist my frantic attempts to wash it out, but as the afternoon progressed the broiling sun baked it onto my head. Even before the baking began, I had dreaded returning to the potato patch; even in Siberia a little girl doesn't want to look like a freak.

Everyone found it amusing—including my parents, after their initial shock at the sight of me—except me. Grandmother had to work at my hair strand by strand, pulling and yanking it, working with her fingers and then with a comb, until every bit of clay was gone.

CHAPTER 5

The first few weeks of life at the gypsum mine had passed and settled into a monotony that seemed as vast and endless as the steppe itself. Torn from sleep by the morning whistle, in the beginning I didn't know where I was, what we were all doing sleeping on a floor with strangers. But soon that too passed and I would slip from sleep to wakefulness, barely noticing the difference. We did what we were told: we worked, we munched bread and cheese—once in a while, as a special treat, we had a bowl of soup with bits of meat in it —we slept. We barely talked.

The fever, or whatever it was I had had, flared up and I spent a few days alone in the room. Someplace Father had found a straw mattress (perhaps with Makrinin's help) and I lay on that—for one day. The next day, when I was in a feverish doze, it was unceremoniously yanked out from under me. Popravka had not learned to love us.

A few nights later, he came in and told us to assemble for a meeting. What now?

We gathered in front of Makrinin's little building and waited. The air was very hot and still and the sky was darkening too quickly. Way off in the distance, there was a flash of light. The crowd stirred. Before long we would be in for it.

There are those who find a Siberian electrical storm very beautiful and exciting. And I imagine it is if one is not scared to death of it. I was, and so were most of the grownups in our midst, it seemed to me. In *our* Siberia, a summer storm was not a summer storm—it was the judgment of God, a God who would punish master and slave alike. The lightning would fork out like a malevolent claw in a frenzy to ground itself on the treeless steppe. The fear was that where there was not a tree in sight, nor a hill, it would ground itself in you if you were outdoors, and quite possibly if you were indoors too. There were times when the huge sky was streaked with lightning wherever you looked.

This sky could be highly dramatic even when there was no storm brewing. At night, I would stand at the window by the hour watching meteors race through the enormous blackness. And there were also those dancing, shifting awesomely beautiful columns of light, the northern lights.

When Makrinin walked out, I hoped he would say

his say quickly, before the storm struck. He did and, to my ten-year-old ears, what he had to say was so unexpectedly exciting that I almost forgot the approaching storm: every Sunday, six people would be allowed to go to the village. Permission would be granted by him, but must be requested well in advance.

Back in our corner of the room, I hastened to assure my parents, before they might have other ideas, that unless I were allowed to go to the village *immediately*, I would *die—immediately*. My poor mother, who was having one of her headaches and whose blistered feet had become so ulcerated that she had to work barefoot, muttered glumly that I was just like my father, always the optimist. Hadn't I learned by now that it was not all that easy to die? My grandmother thought that was a dreadful thing to say to a child—as I did—at which moment the storm broke outside, just in time to interrupt the one that was brewing inside.

Father said that I could have his place and since Mother said that she could not possibly go with her bad feet, Grandmother hastily offered to go as my chaperone. My father suggested that Rubtsovsk was not worth her trudging twelve kilometers each way on a hot dusty road. Grandmother, who had flitted about so gaily in Vilna from dinner party to dinner party, to charity bazaars, theater, and opera, ignored the insinuation that she too was starving for amusement: "What do I care about hot dusty roads? After all, what are grandmothers for?"

We received permission to go in two weeks. When we heard that Rubtsovsk had a market, a *baracholka*, where one could exchange goods for rubles and which

65

was open on Sunday, it was agreed that Grandmother and I should do some trading. Rubles meant food—potatoes perhaps; anything but bread and brinza. We spent every night deciding which of our few belongings we were ready to sell. One of Mother's lace-trimmed French silk slips went in and out of a bag a dozen times. "I really don't need this for dynamiting gypsum," she said.

"Nor do I need this," Father said, holding up a custom-made silk shirt, "for driving a wagon."

Grandmother wasn't so sure they wouldn't need them, and she herself was most reluctant to part with a black silk umbrella with a slender silver handle. "If only we didn't have such nice things . . ." she murmured.

"And what should I part with?" I asked.

"Nothing. You are a growing child," they chorused.

Indeed I was; in those two months—summer being growing time—my skirts already had become almost an inch shorter.

I thought that Sunday would never come. When it did, Grandmother and I set off down the dusty road before anyone else. Along with our wares—the slip, the shirt, and the umbrella, after all—we had wrapped some bread in one of my father's handkerchiefs; the bread was to be our lunch.

It was shortly after six o'clock, the air was still cool and fresh, a hawk was soaring overhead, and, feeling oddly disloyal, I thought that the steppe was just a tiny bit beautiful that morning.

I glanced back over my shoulder. No one was coming after us to order us to return to the mine, but I quickened my pace and urged Grandmother to hurry. "Nonsense!" she said. "We will drop dead if we walk too fast." But she too looked back over her shoulder.

When the mine was out of sight, when there was nothing but Grandmother and me and the steppe, nothing else, not even a hawk in the sky, I didn't shout—I wouldn't dare because of the way sound carried—I didn't sing very loud, but I sang, and my funny little voice sounded strange to me. And I felt light, as if I could do a giant leap over the steppe.

"Grandmother, do you know what?"

"What?"

"We are doing something we *want* to do. All by ourselves. We are fr-r-r-eeeee. . . ."

"Shh!" Grandmother looked around. "Not so loud."

She was dressed in her best dress, a rumpled blue silk that was also beginning to fade, and her little Garbo hat. In spite of her tinyness, Grandmother had always been the *grande dame;* walking down the dusty road that day, she still was.

We walked for about three hours across the uninhabited steppe without meeting one other person. Before long, I had tied my sweater around my waist—my pleated school skirt and blouse had become my uniform—and Grandmother had opened her umbrella.

We saw a bump in the distance. This turned out to be the first of the widely scattered huts, which meant that before too long we would be in Rubtsovsk.

The village had appeared on the horizon like a mirage always receding from us, but we finally did reach it and it was real. Wonderfully real to my starved eyes.

Rubtsovsk, at that time, had an unused church with its onion top, a bank, a library, a pharmacy, a school—

even a movie house and a park with a bandstand. But all I saw that day was a square alive with people and, only vaguely, a rather mean cluster of wooden buildings and huts.

We squeezed our way through the crowd—the men in peaked caps, here and there an old military cap, women in babushkas, friendly faces sometimes scarred from frostbite, friendly voices. And some Kazhaks; Asia at last! Colorful costumes, the women with their long pigtails encased in cloth and leather pouches, and, sad to see, men, women, and children all with rotting teeth. But Kazhaks!

Trading was going on all around us. There were the stalls around the square with produce from the collective farms—and the small farmers too—and there were the buildings with signs proclaiming them to be state-operated stores where one made purchases only if one had been issued ration books, which we had not been. In one corner, sunflower seeds were being roasted over an open fire. The smell was ravishing. "Come on, Grandmother." I nudged her. "Let's begin to trade."

We made our way to the *baracholka*, where wooden horses were set up all over the interior of the square and where piles of stuff were heaped onto blankets or onto the bare stones: old boots, jackets, babushkas, books, pots, pans—anything and everything.

We found a place to stand and, to my surprise, without feeling the least bit self-conscious I immediately held up my mother's slip, the lacy pink silk blowing in the breeze. In a second, we were surrounded: Where were we from? Where did we live? What did Grandmother do? How old was I? They were exceedingly friendly and frankly inquisitive, these native Siberians. We answered the questions as fast as we could, with Grandmother doing most of the talking, since she knew Russian well and I hardly spoke it. We coaxed our potential customers to note the beauty of the lace, the fact that there were 16, *sixteen*, ribs in the umbrella. How much? Forty rubles. *Forty* rubles? There was a roar of laughter. All right, thirty-eight rubles . . . I caught Grandmother's eye; we smiled at each other; we were born traders and we were having a marvelous time. It was, in fact, the happiest time I had had in a long, long time. The guns, the bombs of World War II were thousands of miles away and at the market place so was the labor camp close by. All around me children were giggling over nothing, girls were showing off their dolls— what if they were made of rags?—and boys were wrestling. These children were just like the children in Vilna. Hunger, fatigue, sorrow, and fright were forgotten: haggling was a wonderfully engrossing game. Rough hands that had scrounged in the earth for potatoes, and been frostbitten more than once, fingered the silk, sometimes as if it were a rosary, sometimes as if it were sinful for anything to be that silky, more often to test it for durability. If an egg was around fifteen rubles, how much should a silk slip with *hand-drawn* lace be? Hand drawn, mule drawn, what difference if you couldn't eat it? We all joined in the laughter. I don't remember who bought Father's shirt and Grandmother's umbrella, but the slip was finally bought by a young woman with lots of orange rouge on her cheeks. She was so plump I wondered how she was going to squeeze into it, but that, I decided, was her worry, not mine.

Feeling very proud of ourselves with our newly acquired rubles, we now became the customers. What to buy? We went to the stalls where the produce was—watermelons, cucumbers, potatoes, milk, flour, *white* bread—a great luxury—and meat. Everything was incredibly expensive and we walked back and forth from stall to stall, unable to make a decision. I stood perfectly still in front of the roasting sunflower seeds, ostentatiously breathing in and out. Grandmother counted the rubles we had. "Come," she said, "what are grandmothers for?" The first purchase was a small glassful of sunflower seeds. I slit the shell between my teeth and extracted the tiny nut. I nursed it as if it were a piece of precious candy and it could not have tasted better. Siberians love sunflower seeds and I think ninety percent of them bore a little notch in a front tooth to prove it.

After much deliberation and more bargaining, we bought a piece of meat and a bag of flour. There was a communal outdoor stove at the schoolhouse and we could boil the meat on it and, after mixing the flour with water, we could bake little cakes, the Siberian cakes of our Diaspora.

By that time, the sun had begun to set and Grandmother said we must start our long hike home. But I could tell that she was as reluctant to leave this carnival as I was. So, it seemed, was everyone else. The stalls were empty of their produce; like some kind of game, everyone had everyone else's belongings, wrapped in blankets, coats, babushkas, old flour sacks. But having come together in this vast, lonely steppe, having joked and gossiped and even sung songs, no one wanted to leave.

However, as we began our long trudge back we were very gay, thinking only of the *baracholka*, not of the mine. Grandmother and I had this in common, we were "very" people—either very sad or very gay, with nothing in between. Oh, if we could only live in the village and go to the *baracholka* every Sunday, Siberia would be bearable. I started to tick off the things I had to sell— three dresses, one blouse, a coat. . . Grandmother laughed. "Stop before you go naked in exchange for a glassful of sunflower seeds."

No matter, I thought, whether I had something to sell or not, I would pray that one day we would be allowed to live in the village within sight and sound of the Sunday *baracholka*.

CHAPTER 6

On the steppes of Siberia, fall does not arrive with a great show of flaming leaves; it comes in with a great howling wind. It came during the night in the early part of September and scared me out of my wits. I thought that all the wolves of Siberia had gathered there at the mine to devour us. When Father told me it was only the wind, I said, "What's *only* about it?" Nothing. It began that night and it would continue to blow day in and day out. The temperature began to drop rapidly, and so did our spirits. The prospect of a Siberian winter in this desolate gypsum mine was not a cheery one.

One day we were called to a meeting again. As always, we were filled with apprehension as we gathered in front of Makrinin's building. Poor Makrinin, our original judgment of him had been correct, he was a decent, gentle man stuck with an indecent job.

The sun had already set and people were leaning into the wind, pulling jackets and sweaters closer to their chilled and weary bodies. In the deepening twilight, we could not see Makrinin's face, but he seemed unusually impatient—or excited—as he waved to stragglers to move more quickly into place.

Raising his voice over the wind, he told us that as part of a pact made on the 30th of July between the Soviet Union and Poland, his government granted amnesty "to all Polish citizens now detained on Soviet territory either as prisoners of war or on other sufficient grounds. . . . "

The crowd stirred as he continued.

The amnesty was given at the joint request of the Polish government in exile in London and the government of Great Britian, Russia's ally now in the war against the Germans.

The crowd murmured. I didn't know what an amnesty was, but I could feel the crowd smiling and I knew that at least something good had happened to us Polish deportees.

Makrinin went on to say that we did not have to stay on at the mine, that those of us who wished to could move to the village, where we would be assigned to jobs with a stipend—only a few rubles, to be sure, but nevertheless something.

The crowd sighed. Here and there a man and a woman surreptitiously made the sign of the cross. Someone had remembered us. Way off there in London at a certain hour on a certain day someone had remembered that there were people who were called Polish deportees, someone had remembered that they were *people.* . . .

I hugged Father. "The village! the village!" I said over and over again.

Those who wished to leave? Who in God's name would wish to remain at the mine? Unbelievable as it seemed to us, there were three families who so wished. To some who are homeless, anything—a lean-to, a cave, a doorway—becomes home; what is known is more sheltering, safer, than the unknown. Among the three families who stayed on to endure a Siberian winter were some who did not survive. One young man, in his early twenties, lost his sense of direction in a snowstorm and froze to death only a few yards from the small cluster of buildings.

The rest of us lined up at Makrinin's office. Our turn came and we were assigned to a cart that would leave in three days. We were also told that we would live in barracks on the outskirts of the village. Outskirts? Not *in?* My face must have shown my distress. Makrinin put his hand on my head. "It will be within walking distance," he assured me.

I began to pack and repack my one suitcase immediately. I felt the toes of my beaten-up black school oxfords. My feet were growing fast; I could feel that soon, alarmingly soon, my toes would be all curled up in these shoes. This was the time of year when, home in Vilna, either Miss Rachel or Mother would go shopping with me for school clothes and the first item was always shoes. Would we be able to afford new shoes in Rubtsovsk? I dared not think about it and I decided not to worry my parents about it either.

For the next three days we watched the carts go off. It was like watching people get into lifeboats from a sinking ship. Would the carts come back for us? Would there be a place left for us? Would the amnesty be taken back?

"Just what is an amnesty?" I asked Father. When he told me it was a pardon for a past offense, I fervently hoped that all of us capitalists would be on our best behavior from now on. I went so far as to smile hypocritically at the detestable Popravka. But Popravka had no amnesty in his heart; clearly, Popravka thought that the great and mighty Soviet Union had gone soft on capitalists. It was probably as close to a treasonous thought as he ever allowed himself.

Grandmother had her own question about the amnesty: it would bring Grandfather and her together again, wouldn't it? She reasoned that if it permitted us to travel from the mine to Rubtsovsk, a matter of twelve kilometers, Grandfather with his great wisdom and power would find the way to Rubtsovsk. No one had the heart to suggest that this would call for a miracle. But Grandmother's own faith in Grandfather's ability to accomplish the impossible was such that she began to prepare for this reunion by fussing with her clothes, trying to press the wrinkles out of her dress with her hands, putting her suitcase on top of them and sitting on it, blowing on the little black hat to bring it back to life. Father looked the other way; Mother shook her head; but I too had faith in Grandfather.

Our turn finally came and the only thing that marred our departure from the mine was Boris weeping because he thought he was to be separated from Father. It was impossible to convince him that we would meet at the barracks in another day. His exhausted mother tried to comfort him, but he pushed her away. Father was the most important person in Boris's life then.

As we rode away, Father told us that Makrinin had said good-by to him, that he had wished us luck, and that he had particularly hoped that Mother would be able to get some good attention for her poor feet. We were all rather excessively grateful for a scrap of ordinary decency.

The outskirts proved to be a couple of kilometers from the center of Rubtsovsk and the barracks were indeed barracks—huge wooden crates built in rows. They were not exactly cozy.

However, we were overjoyed to find that among its occupants were some more old friends from Vilna: the Kaftals. Mrs. Kaftal, once a very pretty lady with flirtatious blue eyes, were now smudged with hurt and bewilderment, and her once lovely soft blond curls were dead and discolored. But her daughter Anya was one of the wonders of our exile. Snatched from her home, as we had all been, she had grabbed as her most prized possession her pigskin traveling case fitted out with jars and bottles and vials of creams and soaps and lotions.

The result was truly astonishing: in spite of cattle cars, slave labor camps, starvation, burning heat, and vermin, Anya looked lovely. I was to watch her brush her lashes with mascara in the Siberian dawn before she went off to drudgery at the flour mill; I was to watch her remove the flour from her face with a special cream, the flour from her lashes with a special oil, to tweeze her eyebrows, to bleach a tuft of hair over her lip with peroxide, all by the light of the kerosene lamp we had in our barracks room; I was to watch this with awe. Anya was a goddess whom I never got to know really well, but she had transformed vanity into an act of courage.

Her brother Karl had not been as resourceful. Only his flesh seemed to have survived the cattle car and whatever else the Kaftals had been through.

Except that it had no blackboards, the room was a copy of the one at the schoolhouse, the portraits of Lenin, Marx, Stalin, and Engels apparently having been delivered with the lumber. But here we had *nari*, planks about seventy inches wide set on six legs, lined up on the floor, just barely leaving enough room for entrance and exit. These *nari* may not have been soft as down, but they were beds, one for each family. Some people had straw pads, which they found at the main barracks, and Father said he would try to get some for us. We put our belongings under the bed—we called it our wardrobe from then on—and sat down on the bed with our feet on the floor, the first time in weeks we had been in a normal sitting position. When Father did return with some pads, the thought of sleeping on anything but the bare floor seemed unbelievably luxurious to us. And to me, as I listened to the wind howling outside, the idea of four of us sharing one bed seemed far from a deprivation.

The other luxury was a kerosene lamp; only one, to be sure, for the whole room, but it was the first time since we had left home that the night had any illumination.

The next morning, all the grownups—about thirty or forty—were told to go to the police in the barracks next to ours to receive their orders. The police? What kind of amnesty was this to be? I was left alone to wonder.

And to keep an eye on Boris. No one ever knew for sure, but we liked to think that Makrinin himself had seen how upset Boris was at being parted from Father and had arranged for Mrs. Marshak and Boris to leave earlier than had been planned.

Boris and I went outside, but not for long. The wind was cold and biting that morning and we scurried back to our barracks room, little knowing that that cold wind was like a gentle spring breeze compared to what was to come later. However, I had seen the village in the distance and my spirits rose.

Keeping an eye on Boris was pathetically easy. A half-starved little five-year-old boy didn't have much mischief and curiosity in him. His too-large green eyes kept turning toward the door and he kept asking for Father: "Where's Uncle Samuel? Where did he go?" I could scarcely say, "To the police, to the police, to buy a fat pig."

They came back with the news that they had been assigned jobs: Mother was to work in a bakery, Father on a construction job, Mrs. Marshak and Anya at the flour mill, and Karl on a collective. Grandmother and the other old women and the children were not to work. Neither was Mrs. Kaftal to work—either then or later. The how and why of this would remain among the mysteries of Siberia. Had she persuaded the authorities that they would have a corpse on their hands? Or had she magically recalled for the occasion her old power as a flirt? When she was pressed to explain her luck, her smudged blue eyes became innocent: "Luck? How can you say that? Since you are all to earn some rubles, how will poor little me be able to eat?"

It was a question no one cared to answer.

"Will I go to school?" I asked.

Apparently not, Mother had been told, unless we could find living quarters in the village proper. Some children may have considered the absence of school the most attractive Siberian deprivation of all; not me, I always had loved school. Now I would have another reason for praying that we could move to the village. In Siberia, one thing was certain: one was never at a loss for something to pray for.

Mother, destined to have tough jobs, left for the bakery before dawn. She had to walk about two kilometers in the dark to the bakery, which was close to the village. There she kneaded the heavy and extremely resistant dough and formed it into huge loaves, weighing several kilos, which she lifted in and out of the oven on long-handled shovels. When we expressed sympathy, she brushed us off, saying that at least she was warm and not lonely because there were so many rats. But the job was to have a fringe benefit for me: the workers in the bakery received a larger bread ration—and were frisked every night before they went home to make certain they did not increase it further—and Mother shared some of this bread with me.

Father was more fortunate and, because of Mother, quite embarrassed; he had been given the job of book-keeper at the construction job and had to admit he enjoyed it.

I was bored. For the first time in my life I didn't know what to do with myself. Now my longing for my cousins, my friends, my darling Miss Rachel, became another pain along with that of hunger. I had no books to read, no dolls to play with; as did most of my friends at home, I still loved playing with dolls. Once again there were no children my own age. And poor little Boris, who also had no one to play with, followed me around till I sometimes became very cross with him.

It was still only September, but the wind was bringing colder and colder weather and the steppe was looking more and more desolate. Our rations were very small indeed. We had been issued ration books for use at the state store only. There, we lined up for bread, flour, millet (which tasted ghastly), and occasional treats of sugar, *kukurudza*—a type of corn meal—sunflower-seed oil, or—treat of treats—a piece of meat. Since we had not had a chance to grow our own vegetables, we had no potatoes or carrots or cucumbers, the vegetables that those who had been assigned patches managed to extract from an earth in which permafrost (*vechnaya merzlota*) and selenites were formidable enemies.

One day, when all we had had the day before was a particularly small ration of bread for breakfast, lunch, and supper, I decided to do some hunting on my own. I went out to the cold and windy potato patches, optimistically lugging a blanket for the haul. I carefully explained to Boris, who came along, that I would try to find potatoes that had been *overlooked* by their owners. It was the matter of oversight that automatically invoked the law of finders keepers. Boris nodded; it seemed perfectly logical to him.

We walked slowly between the now barren rows, but the stick in my hand was no hazel switch, had no potato-dowsing properties. There was nothing to do but get down on my hands and knees and crawl along, digging my fingers into the cold, hard earth. Little Boris crawled behind me. Our running noses dripped onto the earth; our fingers nearly froze. Each tiny green potato of dubious worth was a nugget of gold and we let out a whoop of delight. We kept at it for three or four hours.

The whole haul fitted into our pockets, but Father congratulated us on our frontier spirit and told us that we were the stuff that empires were made of. Mother agreed, but suggested that the potatoes had better be cooked and eaten whole or there would be nothing left of them. She was quite right. Under the best of circumstances, peeling potatoes in Siberia was a finicking business; one dared not waste one precious bit of it. As for these poor little sickly things, one slice of the knife and they would have disappeared. Peeling potatoes carelessly, cutting thick peels, became one of my daydreams of the high life.

Hunger also had its fringe benefits: another trip to the *baracholka*. This time the whole family went to sell another slip of Mother's. Grandmother and I were greeted on all sides and, being old hands, showed

Mother and Father the ropes. Once again I had a marvelous time and on this trip we came back with some flour, bread, and a herring. As we had done at the mine, we took our turn at the stove. Here, in addition to the outdoor stove, a primitive tin affair with four holes on top for pots, there was an equally primitive indoor stove. Optimistically, we had brought two pots, four knives, four forks, and four spoons from home, when more times than not all that were needed were our fingers.

My parents found out that we would be permitted to live in the village if we could find living quarters, and one day toward the end of September, after I had nagged and nagged, they decided to start looking. Mother would be nearer the bakery, Father farther away from the construction job, and I would be able to go to school. Mrs. Kaftal, hearing about this, looked more than ever like a little girl lost and Father suggested that she, Anya, and Karl join forces with us.

"What about Boris?" I asked.

Father, the most angelic of men, gave me a look that suggested I was not his little lalinka for asking such a troublesome question. Father had a weakness for saying yes to the first person who came along; he did not like to be reminded of this.

"We will look for a place for Boris and Mrs. Marshak when the time comes," he said. "We haven't found a place yet, have we? Maybe we won't."

I refused to consider the possiblity of such a calamity.

The next Sunday, Sundays being free days, we all put on our best clothes—by which we meant our least dirty and rumpled—and went hut hunting in the village. Obviously, since all huts were occupied we would have to move in with another family.

Mother and Father, both of whom spoke excellent Russian, took turns knocking on doors, only to be told that the places were too small to take us in even if we separated. Being grownups, they found this discouraging and trying, but hungry for any excitement and nosey to boot, I enjoyed peering into the huts, eying the children and being eyed by them.

Finally, we came to a small log hut with a barn in back and chickens scratching at the front door. This time the woman, a sturdy Russian peasant in her late twenties, gave us a quick, shrewd once-over, then smiled in a friendly way and told us to come in and look around.

We filed in, the seven of us, jamming the one room. But *look?* Who could look when one's nose was being assaulted? Yes, assaulted, the hurt traveling rapidly down to the stomach where it became one great big hunger pain. For bubbling away on the stove, sending up a heavenly smell that drowned out all unheavenly smells, was a peasant soup: *the real thing—meat* and potatoes and carrots and cabbage and onions and salt and pepper. My nose picked out the ingredients, one by one.

When I managed to tear my eyes from the soup pot —everyone else was similarly affected and Mrs. Kaftal appeared to be on the verge of fainting or weeping—I thought that the room was really quite pretty. A flowered cretonne curtain hung across one wall like a tester for the high-heaped featherbed on which lay huge, plump pillows. A scrubbed deal table and two chairs were set between two tiny windows, and the black iron stove not only brewed magic but made the place cozy.

The woman pointed to the bare wall opposite the bed and said that they hoped that one day soon it would be occupied by a baby, but until that time it might just as well be used by—she counted us off—seven people. "How much money can you pay?" she asked. Father told her that his and Mother's wages together came to ninety or one hundred rubles and the Kaftals' somewhat less. Would twenty-five rubles for us and twenty for the Kaftals do? She would fetch her husband from the barn; he would decide.

Left alone in the room, we were silent.

"Stop breathing so hard," Father said. "After all, it's not Mama's roast duck."

"Or cutlets Kiev . . ." Mrs. Kaftal whimpered.

"Will we be able to stand it if we live here?" Mother asked.

"We have endured worse," Father said. "Courage, everyone . . ."

"Maybe . . . maybe . . . they will share." I suggested

They looked at me as if I were crazy.

"*Sometimes* . . ." I persisted.

The woman came back with her husband, who could have been her brother so alike were they except for his eyes, which were squinting and oozing matter. (Inadvertently, Mother pulled me closer to her.) Yes, yes, he shouted cheerfully, it was a deal. We could make two beds for ourselves along the wall and he and father should have a drink on it. He brought out a bottle of real vodka, not cologne, and one glass. Mother looked worried, but Father looked delighted. The man introduced himself: his name was Nikita Alexandrovich and his wife was Nina Ivanovna, but we were to call them Nina and Nikita. Father hesitated. I could see that he was uncertain about the etiquette of the situation; in our world, first names were reserved for the family and only the very closest friends. In spite of being practically bedfellows, Mrs. Kaftal and Mrs. Marshak were never addressed by their first names, nor were my parents and grandmother thus addressed by them. With his most ingratiating smile and a little bow, Father introduced us as the Rudomins and the Kaftals. Nina and Nikita returned the bows. Nikita poured a full glass of vodka and handed it to father.

"Samuel—not on an empty stomach," Mother whispered.

Father smiled blandly and took a draught. "I cannot return the hospitality, therefore I beg of you . . ." Father bowed again and handed the rest of the vodka back to Nikita.

Nikita did not press the point and finished off that glass and a second one, wiping his mouth with one great sweep. His eyes disappeared completely as he gave us and the rest of the world an indulgent grin.

Nikita said he would borrow a horse and buggy from the mill where he worked and he would fetch us the next evening.

I felt almost ill with excitement and joy. Now I would be in the village, I would go to school, and . . .

"You see, " I said, the minute we were out of earshot, "Nikita *does share*——"

"Share? That's just what I'm afraid of. Samuel, doesn't he have trachoma?" Mother asked. "When he brought out that *one* glass— Honestly, Samuel, I think you would drink poison if it was offered to you, before you would hurt someone's feelings."

Father, warmed by the vodka, imitated Nikita's grin. "Don't worry, if I am a judge of Nikita, fine fellow though he is, he will not offer me any more vodka. He assumes that his need is greater than mine. And as for the trachoma—we will all be very careful. Nina doesn't have it, does she? So let us stop all this worrying and let us be grateful that we are to move from the barracks."

Mother promised to be grateful, but she gave me a long lecture on how I was not to use anything belonging to Nikita—no towel, no soap if there was any—nothing, *nothing*, did I hear her? With a child's ears, I had gone deaf after the first sentence or two, but I said yes, yes, *yes*, that I had heard her.

"And no vodka either, lalinka," Father said, putting his arm around me. "Lalinka . . ."

The next evening, when everyone had come back from work, we waited for Nikita, the seven of us, with our bags and bundles once again the symbol of our exile. There was no moon that night and we found a place close to the faint light from the barracks. How else would Nikita find us, Mother worried? We will find *him*, Father reassured her rather testily. How many carts would appear out of the night? he wanted to know. Mrs. Kaftal, listening to them quibbling as husbands and wives seem always to do on the eve of a trip, even on the steppes of Siberia, was overcome with loneliness for her Alfred: she too wanted a husband to quibble with. They had been separated in the same insane way that Grandmother and Mrs. Marshak had been separated from their husbands. "What bliss it would be," she said, "to have a rousing good fight with Alfred." As we all laughed, I thought it was going to be jolly living together with the Kaftals.

Soon we heard the clop of horse's hoofs and in the darkness we could see the outline of a wagon. Then a match flared; Nikita had lit a lantern. We piled into the low-slung, long, narrow cart with its slanting sides and snuggled under our blankets for the short but very cold ride in the dark. Cold or no cold, I loved every minute of it; after all, it was a ride in a horse and wagon and I was sorry when it was over.

Nina greeted us warmly and told us that since we didn't have *nari* yet, she would put some straw on the floor for us. Later, she would help us to make some straw mattresses for our *nari*. She also warned us that we were to use the kerosene lamp as little and as carefully as possible since not only was oil scarce, but so were wicks.

We made some dough out of flour, water, and salt and rolled it out on Nina's scrubbed table—her hut was clean by any standards and remarkably clean for Siberia —formed it into the usual cakes, and baked them on the stove. That night they didn't have the usual flat taste, that night they were delicious; one could not have gotten a better cake at Stral's, the finest café in Vilna. Nina brought me a glass of milk and I shot Mother a look that said, See? I told you so. Even though the milk was slightly bitter from the Siberian grass, it was *milk* and I drank it. However, I did pour some of it into the hot water the rest were going to have, making their drink at least resemble tea with milk.

We were content. It was even good to hear the wind howling outside, enhancing the coziness inside.

We dressed the straw with sheets and blankets and called out good night to each other as if there were nothing in the least remarkable about seven people sharing a room with two strangers. But Nina and Nikita must have found much to discuss about our presence, because I could hear them whispering long into the night.

CHAPTER 7

When I woke up the next morning, Mother had already left for the bakery and Nina and Nikita were about to breakfast on their thick peasant gruel. They greeted me with perfect friendliness, but without any embarrassment whatsoever they ate their good thick peasant gruel, dunked their bread into milk, and watched me eat my piece of dry black bread. This was the way it was to be: there was a time for sharing and a time for not sharing, and no sentimental nonsense about it.

Just before Nina left for work, she looked at me for a second as if there was something on her mind, something she wanted to ask me; then apparently she thought better of it and merely asked me when Mother would come home.

Left alone, Grandmother and I did some exploring. There wasn't much to see on Nina and Nikita's place: a cow, a pig, and some chickens made up their livestock and the kitchen garden had been almost completely harvested, except for a cabbage or two, and was beginning to freeze.

Like a pair of puppies breaking tether, we went farther afield. We came upon a creek, and, seeing some wooden planks bridging it, we walked them. But all we got to was the other side, so we returned. I was to become very familiar with this creek. Not only would I wash clothes in it, but I would go down to it with two pails strung across my shoulders and a third pail in my hand and return with them filled. And when the creek froze, Father took his turn at breaking the ice, not only a strenuous task but a dangerous one—a misstep and one could drown in the icy waters.

We went past the *baracholka*, which was very quiet that day, and came to what was unquestionably the most elegant part of the village, where raised boardwalks served as a street for those who were lucky enough to live alongside them in larger wooden houses with whitewashed shutters. Walking these boards, we went past the bank, a small building which we identified as the library, and a substantial white building which might once have been a church and which now was the local movie theater.

Walking beside my grandmother through this stark village, I walked in an unreal world—unfurnished and unpeopled.

That evening, when Mother came home from the bakery, Nina, who had already eaten, was plainly impatient for her to finish her bread. Having only one table and two chairs, we ate in shifts; but with our austere menu, speed was no problem.

"Can you milk a cow?" Nina asked Mother.

Mother, whose face was greenish from fatigue, said she couldn't but that she was willing to try. Nina good-naturedly refused this offer; Mother might be willing, but not the cow. In fact, the cow would be sure to kick such a beginner. But wouldn't Mother like to keep her company in the barn?

Mother, who knew that Nina had more on her mind than company, went out with her.

When Nina and Nikita were in bed and Nikita's snores drowned our whispering, Mother told us what it was all about. Nina longed for a cross and since crosses were not exactly plentiful in Soviet society, the longing had become unbearable. Mother must please give Nina her cross. But we don't wear crosses, Mother told her. Nina thought it was because we feared the police and promised not to tell. When Mother told her that we were Jews, Nina stubbornly insisted that that was impossible since all Jews had crooked noses and the men wore long beards. No matter how hard Mother tried, Nina remained unconvinced and even somewhat suspicious: what were these people up to, pretending that they were Jews when anyone could see that they weren't?

All in all, life at Nina and Nikita's was not dull. There were their violent quarrels and their passionate reconciliations. There was the wheel of fortune—who was to be the lucky winner? the one to get the occasional bowl of real soup or a slab of meat from Nina?

(Grandmother and I, being the oldest and the youngest, were the luckiest.) And there was a rather odd social custom: it consisted of nit picking and it was usually done after a nice cup of hot tea.

The first time I witnessed it, I was invited to participate and I politely accepted. A friend visited Nina one afternoon when I was alone with her. They had their cup of tea and their gossip and then Nina's friend, a pleasant lady around Nina's age, placed her head in Nina's lap and had it deloused. The instrument was a knife, and Nina, being a tidy housekeeper, parted her friend's heavy head of hair so that the knife was used on every inch of scalp. When Nina was finished, her friend returned the compliment: Nina put her head on her friend's lap. My turn was last and I laid my head on Nina's lap. It was all very cozy, and a nice change.

And there was the matter of the missing bread.

We kept what food we had under the *nari* that Father and Nikita had built—one for us and one for the Kaftals. One day Grandmother unwrapped our lunch ration of bread. "I thought your mama brought us a much bigger piece of bread than this." I studied the piece of black bread resting on Father's handkerchief and agreed that it seemed to have shrunk considerably overnight. Could it be mice or rats that had gotten at it? we asked each other, knowing that they could not have untied and retied the kerchief.

"Who could have stolen some?" I asked.

Grandmother said we weren't to think such thoughts, that funny things happened to people when they were hungry and probably it was all our imagination. But I saw her eyes stray to Nina's bed. That would be too terrible, I thought. With all the food they had compared to us—milk, vegetables, meat, tea! Nevertheless, I was pleased to see Grandmother tuck the supper ration away with extra care.

The next day or two nothing seemed to be missing, but one day when our appetites had been appallingly stimulated by the smell of a juicy stew on the stove, there was no mistaking it: a big slice of bread was missing. "Shouldn't we go to the police?" I asked Grandmother.

"God forbid!" she retorted.

But she was very much upset and that night in bed there was much whispering with Mother and Father. As a devotee of mysteries, I fancied myself an expert and wanted to put my two cents in, but I was told that this was not a matter for little girls and that I was to go to sleep. Little girl indeed! Since Mother had to work at the bakery, I was doing all sorts of grown-up things like cleaning, cooking, and going to the *baracholka*. I was outraged.

In the morning, we were diverted. The first snow had come to the Siberian steppes. I was enchanted. Siberia or no Siberia, snow was snow and in our family we loved it. Mother and Father were great skiers and were always going off to Zakopane, a skiing resort in Poland. And Miss Rachel used to take Musik and me sledding, the two of us dressed in our sealskin-lined coats and our black sealskin hats, mine a little round one tied under my chin with white wool ribbons and Musik's a little peaked cap with ear muffs. (All the furs, Mother's coats and Father's fur-lined coat, had been inaccessibly stored away that June day.) Vilna with its trees and parks and red-tiled roofs was particularly ravishing in the snow.

Peering out the window of the hut, I saw that the muddy roads had disappeared and that Rubtsovsk had been made beautiful by the snow.

"But it's only October," Grandmother complained, implying that in Siberia they just couldn't do anything right.

This time, Mother didn't find the snow enchanting either. "Esther has no boots. What will she wear?" None of us had boots. "And her coat isn't warm enough." There was a note of panic in her voice and for once Father looked deeply worried too.

Even Nina looked guilty as she pulled on her *pimy* boots, the knee-length felt boots that were to become our most desperate need. "It's only a light snow," she said. "This is nothing—"

Tact was not one of her virtues.

Mrs. Kaftal wondered why we could not have been told to prepare ourselves for Siberia, everyone would have been so much more comfortable, wouldn't they? with their nice fur coats? and their good boots? what harm would it have done anyone? Karl, who rarely spoke, told his mother to shut up so sharply that we all felt the sting.

My shoes seemed exceptionally tight and flimsy that morning. But as soon as Mother and Father had gone, I went outside. The snow might be light, but it had completely covered the steppe. Now, at last, this was Siberia.

It was at this moment that I fell in love with *space*,

endless space. And since Siberia was space, I had to include it—just a little and with great guilt—in this love.

I picked up some snow and rubbed it on my face, tasted it with my tongue. Vilna! Miss Rachel! Musik! My cousins! I was only eleven years old and it was all too much for me. I ran back into the hut.

The night before Mother was to take me to school, I was the center of attention: Anya omitted one of her beauty steps in order to brush my hair long and hard, fruitlessly trying to bring back some of its life; Grandmother cut my nails and pushed *my* cuticles back; and Mother borrowed an iron from Nina, heated it on the stove, and pressed my blouse and skirt. And Nikita good-naturedly reminded us that oil and wicks ought not to be wasted on an eleven-year-old girl, but saved for when she was sixteen and in need of a husband.

"Speak Russian to me, Mama," I asked, cuddling up to her in bed.

"Once upon a time . . ." she began in Russian, "there was a little girl who . . ."

I waited. "Who what?" I asked impatiently in Polish.

"Speak Russian . . ." Mother muttered and fell sound asleep. Her day at the bakery didn't leave her with any energy for the children's hour.

But I did not sleep. What child going to any new school does? And if the school is in the wilds of Siberia? And if the child is a deportee, some kind of a capitalist where no kind is good, what then? And much as I had always loved school, there was the business of not knowing Russian well, of not making friends easily, of not having cousins to fall back on—no Musik to protect me, no Musik who always used to let me win at hopscotch. The night was bringing more worries than I cared for.

I thought morning would never come, and when it came I thought it would never end. Mother was to be given an extra hour for lunch to take me to school for my interview. Waiting for her, I practiced Russian: "*Zdrastvuytie*, my name is Esther Rudomin, what is yours? I am eleven years old. How old are you? What is your favorite subject? Who is your favorite movie star? . . ." Fortunately, I didn't know the Russian for "None of your business, Miss Busybody."

The school was a surprise. In the midst of the drab clutch of buildings that was Rubtsovsk in 1941, here was something worthy of a picture postcard. Sparkling white clapboard; crystal-clear windows; gingerbread carved under the eaves; and, as befitted the pride of Rubtsovsk, its prize jewel, a white picket fence to set it apart.

"Oh, it's so beautiful—" I sighed as if I were about to enter an enchanted castle. "What should we do with our shoes?" I looked down at our wet and mud-encrusted shoes. It would be too awful to dirty this marvel of beauty and cleanliness; even worse to be scolded for it. In the hut, we all took off our shoes before entering and placed them on the stove to dry, the custom of the land in private homes.

Mother thought about it. Then she spotted a broom and we swept each other's shoes clean.

Inside, the building looked much the same as the schoolhouse in which we had lived at the mine. The wide empty corridor with the portraits of Lenin, Stalin, Marx, and Engels. And off it, the classrooms with doors open to catch whatever little heat came from a centrally placed stove. And there the resemblance ended. Instead of a barracks strewn with bags and bundles and baskets, it was a schoolhouse. The rooms were crowded with desks at which children sat wearing their coats and hats and, in some cases, their mittens. Physically, the building was certainly cold, but to me, starving not only for food but for school and children my age, this place was like a blaze inviting me to come close. Suddenly I began to feel a little warmth in this ice-cold Siberia.

Tiptoeing down the empty corridor in search of the principal's office, I caught a phrase of a lesson in math and I became anxious. Math was difficult enough for me in Polish; what would it be like in Russian?

The principal was an elderly woman with rough gray hair pulled back from a melancholy face. Her sad eyes sized us up and came to rest for a second on our shabby wet shoes. She rose to greet us with a little smile—of sympathy? Perhaps. In any case, we were being treated like human beings. We shook hands and I teetered on the edge of the curtsy we used in Vilna; uncertain about its appropriateness in Siberia, it ended up more like a nervous wiggle.

Mother gave the principal the vital statistics about me and I watched the principal's face to see where these statistics were going to land me.

"She will go into the fifth grade," the principal said.

I was much relieved. That was my proper grade; I was not to be left back, that Siberia of all Siberias to children.

"Has she studied foreign languages in Poland?"

Mother told her that we did not learn any at school but that my governess had taught me German and that I had also learned Yiddish.

"Here she will have a choice of German, French, or English."

Mother raised an eyebrow. "A foreign language in the fifth grade in a . . ."

"Little school in Siberia?" the principal finished mother's sentence. "Yes, it is our simple ambition to educate our children, all of them."

Mother expressed her admiration and it was decided that I would continue with my German. Since this was the language I had spoken so often with Miss Rachel, I had mixed feelings about it—traitorous, too?—but I kept them to myself.

Then the principal said that since supplies were running very low at the school, she could give me only one notebook for the time being. "Later, she will have to get her own. How she will do this I do not know, but somehow it must be done." She and mother shook their heads in mutual dismay. (Later, I was to use old newspapers, writing between the lines.) "And . . ." the principal continued, "I must also tell you that there are no more textbooks left. She will have to do her studying with another child. It is this terrible war——"

"Please don't apologize," Mother said. "It will be good for her to share the books of another child. It will help her to make friends."

Many times in Siberia, I would wake up not knowing

where I was, sometimes not certain I was truly awake, sometimes not even certain I knew who I was.

The morning I was to go to school for the first time, I woke up in a blackness that was as mysterious as the heart of a dark forest and as if the sounds close by were its strange beat. But the howl of a wolf way out on the steppe gave me my bearings. The strange beat was the breathing of my parents, my grandmother, the Kaftals, and Nina and Nikita. They breathed, they sighed, they snored, they caught their breath suddenly through their noses with comical gurgles. Sometimes they talked or called out. "Solomon!" my grandmother would cry. It was noisy in the hut at night.

I leaned over and ran my fingers over my notebook and the stub of pencil that Karl Kaftal had contributed. How long would they last? How small could I write?

I crept out of bed, got into my underclothes which had been kept warm in the comforter, and throwing my coat on, went shivering to the outhouse. I had never been out this early. The moon and the stars were still bright and clear and the steppe was bewitched. I looked up at the moon and I prayed for some friends at school; for fear that I was being greedy, I amended the plural —just *one* girl, please, to play with. Or, if Musik would forgive me, one boy would do almost as well.

That morning, in honor of the occasion, Nina gave me a glass of warm milk.

I dressed as warmly as I could, although deep winter had not yet arrived, with a pull-over sweater (which was to become like a second skin in the next years) over my blouse, my one and only coat, and the black leather oxfords which were not only pinching but which were beginning to crack from the wet and the mud and the stove. Would we be able to sell something and buy ourselves some *pimy* boots? Would there be any to buy? The question was becoming more and more serious. We had begun to recognize the signs of frostbite—the scarred faces, the shuffle of feet minus some toes.

Mother had to be at the bakery and, clutching my notebook and pencil, I went to school alone. It never occurred to me that for a child to walk down a Siberian road, in every possible way the outsider—from the tips of her inappropriate shoes to her tongue stumbling over the language—required some courage. I was too busy trying to review the Russian alphabet.

On the way, I was distracted by a pattern in the snow; it looked something like hopscotch and I hopped through it in the hopscotch way.

Though I arrived very early, some other children had beaten me to it. I saw them in the classrooms gossiping and teasing each other. With my Russian suddenly become more broken than usual, I asked a boy I met in the hall where classroom number five was. In a very loud voice, he asked me if I was a new girl. Although I had understood the question perfectly, I shrugged. "You don't know?" he asked with understandable surprise. I blushed and hastened toward the room he pointed to.

In room number five, a few children in caps and coats were seated at their desks watching the teacher write on the blackboard. She turned when I came in and looked at me so severely my heart sank. In addition, her close-cropped hair and short, stocky figure gave a strong impression of sullen stubbornness.

"You are Esther Rudomin. From Poland. Your Russian is poor." It was as if she were reading from a dossier that would determine my punishment. "It will be my task to see that you improve it. My name is Raisa Nikitovna. Go to the last desk of the third row and sit down."

"Thank you."

Last desk of the third row . . . one . . . two . . . three . . . In my anxiety not to make a mistake, I almost went to the fourth row, but caught myself in time.

I placed the notebook and the pencil on the center of the desk and waited. The other children began to file in and take their places, eying me with frank curiosity as they did so. I was not quite so frank; I kept my eyes lowered, but not so much that I could not do some sizing up myself. I recognized one or two children from the *baracholka*, and on the whole they looked like a redcheeked, cheerful group, sturdy survivors of the hard Siberian life.

When the bell rang, everyone stood up, bowed to Raisa Nikitovna, and called, "Good morning, Raisa Nikitovna," in unison.

"Good morning, children."

Without another word, she picked up a book, called out a page number. It was a fable by the Russian writer Ivan Krylov, and everyone had a book but me. The feeling must have been something like being the only soldier without a gun. I leaned toward the girl next to me and asked if I might share her book. She grudgingly agreed. She was a very pretty girl with short blond curly hair and eyes the special blue of northern countries. I asked her name but she told me to be quiet, that there was absolutely no talking at all allowed in class.

My first lesson in school in Siberia was memorable for being a chilly one. Not only did Krylov evade me, lost as he was in a sea of Cyrillic letters, but so did the book itself—literally. My classmate somehow managed to keep slipping it out of my field of vision, which forced me to strain, squirm, and nudge her to bring the book closer. Naturally, I had barely read the first paragraph when Raisa Nikitovna began to quiz the class. To my horror, one question was directed at me. Fortunately— or with more humanity than I was giving that severe-faced woman credit for—it concerned the opening of the fable. As I began to answer in my halting Russian, all the children turned to stare at me; I braced myself against the derisive laughter I expected. But no one laughed. As I was to learn, discipline was no problem in the Siberian classroom, none whatsoever. In that harsh country, going to school was a privilege no one wanted to monkey with.

When the lesson was finished, Raisa Nikitovna introduced me to the class: "This is Esther Rudomin, who comes from Poland. As you can tell, she does not know Russian well and she will have to work hard to catch up. She will share her books with Svetlana. Stand up, Svetlana."

Svetlana turned out to be the pretty little girl sitting next to me; the prospect of *sharing* with her was not heartening. However, I made a prim little speech thanking Raisa Nikitovna and promising to study hard. Would we be learning Russian grammar, of which I knew very little? I inquired. Raisa Nikitovna was not impressed by little eager beavers; she snapped back that most certainly we would study Russian grammar—one day grammar, one day poems and stories. What kind of a school did I think I had come to? her tone implied.

I sat down.

Happily the bell rang just then and I discovered that in this school one had a short recess between classes, since it was the teachers who moved from classroom to classroom, not the children. I was immediately surrounded by children firing questions at me which I had trouble understanding and answering: Did I really come from Poland? Where was Poland? What did people speak there? Was it cold there in the winter? In spite of the difficulty with the language, this much attention from my classmates felt more like the strokes of little velvet paws than a barrage.

The bell rang again and a wizened, dwarflike man came in. Once again the children snapped to attention, rose to their feet, and bowed. This time I bowed, too. This man taught mathematics, which would now become not only difficult but impossible. He spoke so low that I could barely hear him and scribbled things on the blackboard that were equally unintelligible to me. When the lesson was over and he had assigned a great deal of homework, I asked Svetlana what would happen if I couldn't do it all. She cheerfully told me that I better had do it, since this teacher was the biggest terror of them all. If there was one thing I didn't need, I thought, it was one more terror in Siberia.

As the day went on, I met the men and women who were to teach us German, history, and geography. I learned that here one was graded from one to five—with the usual plus and minus—one being complete failure, two worse than a D, and five being excessively difficult to attain and practically worthy of the Order of Lenin. I learned that the school year was from September through May with a holiday at the New Year and one week off to help with the spring planting.

History was taught with some curious omissions, one being the late tsar. He simply disappeared from history; not once were his execution and that of his family ever mentioned by the teacher. Nor by me, I might add. Without too much instruction from my parents, I had learned that in Siberia one had better not be a show-off. I would as soon have instructed my classmates in the facts about the tsar—or capitalism, if I had understood it—as I would have offered my head for the block. I had no interest in being a heroine, let alone a martyr.

But there was one great fringe benefit to the study of history: along with our studies of Peter the Great, Catherine, Rasputin, the French Revolution, the Russian Revolution, the Industrial Revolution, we read the appropriate novels. We read Aleksei Tolstoi's *Peter the Great*, we read Dumas, we read Balzac, we read Dickens (as an example of how terrible capitalism was), we read about Spartacus. . . . We read, we read, we read.

Since I was to study with Svetlana, she was the most likely person to become my friend. But the more attention I got, the more she sulked. I sensed that Svetlana was the queen bee and that I had become her natural enemy. This was confirmed when I asked if I might come to her house to study with her. The answer was a sharp "No!" I would be allowed to fetch the books in the evening when she was quite finished with them, but

I could jolly well trot myself home and study alone.

At the end of my first day at school, I collapsed on the *nari*. Out of the confusion of the day, three giants emerged to be slain: Svetlana, Raisa Nikitovna, and Krylov in Cyrillic letters. In that order.

I did not know that in the wings there were one or two more awesome ones waiting for me.

CHAPTER 8

One day a piece of cheese was missing.

I was sitting at the table, struggling with my homework, and Grandmother and Mrs. Kaftal were on the Kaftals' *nari* engaged in their favorite competition, the remembrance of things past. Who had the most trouble with the servants? Whose husband had the more extravagant taste in jewels? Whose husband killed himself more at his work? was fussier about his shirts? knew the best restaurant in Warsaw? Eyes bright, heads bobbing, these two artists re-created the past as if they were forging armor for their knights.

I was into my second month at school. The past, World War II, and exile were of far less consequence to me than the problem of x: if y = such and such, and z = such and such, everyone but me would know what x equaled. I was finding the work exceedingly difficult, the teachers strict, and Svetlana more unfriendly as the other children continued to be friendly and inquisitive. But I had not become one of them. I had come from fairyland as far as they were concerned. Although I had been wily enough to demote father to "some sort of engineer," I had been too explicit about upper-middle-class life in Vilna, and my clothes, shabby as they had become, were of much better quality than theirs. Incongruously, as I had sometimes been in the school in Vilna, here too I was the pariah poor little rich girl, the outsider. To be one of them became my greatest ambition; my next greatest ambition was to do well at my work; other ambitions, such as to be a famous writer, were temporarily overshadowed.

"Don't talk so loud!" I begged as x refused to reveal itself.

"She's hungry," Grandmother apologized to Mrs. Kaftal. "Have a little something to eat, Esther."

It was early for supper, but I too thought a piece of brinza might help. I fetched it from the hamper under our bed and discovered that at least half of it was gone. I cried out.

"*Again?*" Grandmother was close to hysteria. "What will we do?"

"Go to the police!" I shouted, not caring who heard me.

"No! No! No!" Mrs. Kaftal had jumped off the bed.

Grandmother and I stared at her. True, we all feared the police, but her face had become violently red and she was trembling from head to toe.

I couldn't look at her.

There was a dreadful silence and then Grandmother said, "Oh, stop imagining things, Esther, nothing's missing. Take a piece of cheese and go back to your homework."

I did as I was told. I felt hideously embarrassed, as if it were *I* who had been caught.

"My husband was always very particular about the governesses for his grandchildren . . ." Grandmother went on in a brave voice.

But Mrs. Kaftal pleaded a headache and Grandmother tiptoed back to her own bed.

It was not the end of missing food. From time to time it would happen again and when it did we all held our tongues, as if the hunger that provoked the theft was a fatal illness to be kept secret from the patient.

Trouble was our constant dark companion.

I had begun to cough. At night in the hut, I tried to stifle the cough, but the harder I tried, the more I coughed. Nina and Nikita slept on apparently undisturbed, but the others would stir restlessly. And my parents and grandmother began to fret: no cough medicine, not even milk and honey, no *boots*.

My cough became more persistent and the walk to and from school longer and longer, what with the paroxysms of coughing and the need to recover my breath from them. Mother heard that there was a very good woman doctor in the village, one of the new refugees from Moscow. The German siege of Russia had begun.

Her office was in the village infirmary, and it was not very attractive. But she wore a white coat and a stethoscope, and with her hair parted in the middle and drawn back into a bun, she was the prototype of the Russian woman doctor. The second she cupped my chin with her broad hand and looked into my face, I liked her and trusted her. She listened to my chest, my back, took my temperature, my pulse. She had no X-ray machine, there was no laboratory for blood tests, perhaps she would find a microscope to do a sputum test, but she was certain of the diagnosis: a severe bronchitis which must not be neglected or— With their eyes, she and Mother finished the sentence together.

I was to be put to bed immediately.

"But my schoolwork . . . I'm having enough trouble as it is. . . ."

The doctor shook her head. "There is to be no trouble with schoolwork. There is to be no school. There is to be only rest. Only rest and no trouble." She smiled sadly at Mother. "No trouble . . ."

"*No school?* Until when?"

"We'll see. Mostly likely not before spring."

"*Spring?* But I'll be left *behind*. . . ." I wailed.

The doctor put her arm around me. "Already you are not obeying doctor's orders. I said no trouble, no worry. No worry is the best medicine for you. No worry and rest, rest, rest. The body and the mind. It is the only medicine we have—and we are going to use it." Again she looked at Mother. "Whenever possible—milk, eggs—" As if she had committed an egregious social blunder, she blushed and stopped herself. But more than once during that long, long winter this doctor would pay her call carrying with her an egg or a jug of milk or a jar of broth.

And so I was to stay in the hut that first Siberian winter. It was there that I had my first personal confrontation with tragedy.

The knock on the door came in the early evening. It

was another deportee, fresh from a labor camp, a former lawyer, a prominent one—everyone had been prominent once. The man came to the point in his own time. It was cold in the labor camp, many people were sick. With no care, no medication, they died like flies, but there were trees to be chopped down. He had been sick, very sick—*who* had been sick?—and he had been ordered to chop trees, an old man with pneumonia. It was his sad mission to tell Grandmother——

Grandmother screamed.

For myself, my own love for my grandfather had figured so strongly in the pattern of my life up until then that I did not know what to do with my sense of loss, my grief, and my terror.

White-faced and grim, his eyes blazing with anger as well as grief, my father began the ritual mourning for his father. How this was accomplished I do not know, but morning and evening ten Jewish men gathered in the hut, having trudged through the wind and the cold before and after God knows what labors, to say the prayer for the dead. Father, who had had rabbinical training, led the services.

These men covered their heads with whatever was at hand—a hat, a cap, a *yarmulka* that had been grabbed in flight, a handkerchief, a rag—and turned toward Jerusalem: "*Yis-gad-dal v'yis-kad-dash.*" —Magnified and sanctified be His name. The beautiful Kaddish.

On the third night, quite unceremoniously the door burst open. It was the police. The ten men turned and stood still.

Did they know that to run a synagogue was against the law? And subject to punishment?

They were not running a synagogue.

Oh, no? Then what *were* they doing?

They were mourning their dead.

What dead?

The services were interrupted. Father went to the chief of police. What proof did he have that his father was dead? The chief of police was not easily persuaded. Father went away with the strong impression that there had better be no more communal services for any reason, that the Jewish community was now suspect.

For seven days Grandmother sat *shivah* alone except for Mrs. Kaftal and me. Once or twice another old woman adrift in Siberia came to pay her respects. At home during this period, Grandmother would have been surrounded by her family, and friends would have come and gone to help her through the initial stage of shock. In Siberia, she endured the seven days of mourning stretched out on the *nari*, seeming to be herself barely alive. Every once in a while she would say something to reveal that she was lying there reliving the days of their courtship, their marriage, their truly great love for each other. ". . . That was the day he brought me violets, the big purple ones . . . Karlsbad . . . like in a romance . . ." " . . . every morsel he ate I tasted first . . . you think, my Solomon would say, it was the kitchen of the Borgias and my wife suspected poison . . ."

Traditionally, the *yahrzeit* candle for the dead should have burned throughout the period of mourning, but there were no candles; instead, Grandmother was allowed to turn the kerosene lamp low and keep it burning throughout the night. Oil and wicks were scarce, but

Nina and Nikita had great respect for ritual and tradition. There were some others who had it too: old women were sometimes to be seen surreptitiously carrying bread under their shawls to be blessed by a former priest.

When the eight days were over, Grandmother went out onto the steppe and disappeared for hours. As I remained in the hut waiting for her to return, I imagined that I still heard her cries.

That night the first Siberian storms came. It seemed impossible that the force of the turbulence, churning over thousands of miles of steppe, would not carry the tiny hut away with it. Not far away from us, the roof of another hut caved in that night. The windows of ours had iced over, but peering through a crack in the door, seeing nothing but the never-ending swirling snow, one had a sense of tumbling through space in total isolation.

There were many such storms that winter. The first few times I watched my parents bundle themselves into grotesque figures with whatever was available—fortunately they had bought some old cheaply patched *pimy* boots at the *baracholka*—and go out into the snow, I was justifiably terrified that I would never see them again.

Mother quickly learned some techniques for protecting herself. She learned the Siberian way of wrapping her crocheted shawl over her head and across her face, leaving only one eye exposed. She said that with everyone dressed this way, out on the steppe you could go right past your own child unless there was something distinctive about the shawl. The lashes of the exposed eye—or eyes if the cold permitted—froze with a little white crust on them, which I thought was very pretty. Wearing glasses, of course, was out of the question.

She also learned that goose fat was a necessity. After her first bout with frostbite—the flesh first white as pork fat, then purple—she managed to get hold of some goose fat and smeared it over her face, fingers, and toes. Even so, she still suffered subsequent attacks, particularly on her fingers.

Much as I loved the snow, I did not feel deprived when I was forbidden to go out into these maelstroms —except when it was necessary to use snowshoes, which Mother and Father improvised out of slabs of wood.

As the weeks and months went by and the snow piled up, sometimes nearly obliterating a hut, the isolation one felt in a Siberian hut was more than separation or loneliness, it was almost like an additional sense that one had been born with and would never lose.

I had no one, and nothing, to play with, nothing to read except an occasional book Anya borrowed from the library in Rubtsovsk.

When the weather would not permit Grandmother to take her misery out onto the steppe, she lay on the *nari* with it hour after hour, day after day, through that first Siberian winter.

CHAPTER 9

Nina announced that she was going to have a baby and we would have to move. Happy news for her and bad news for us. It was not merely that we had gotten used to living with these friendly people, but housing had become an extremely serious problem. By now, more and more people were fleeing from the German armies in European Russia and crowding into the Siberian villages.

Everyone took turns hunting. Even I was allowed to go out when it was not too cold—a relative term if ever there was one—or stormy, and at last we found a place on the other side of the village. Nina and Nikita's clean and cheerful hut was a dream house by comparison. This dingy little hut with its two tiny dark rooms was occupied by two dour sisters and an equally dour little boy. We were told that we could move in temporarily (a word more promising than threatening to our ears); we were to provide half the heating material for the hut; and the rent was to be double the amount we had paid Nikita. For this largesse, it was also necessary to receive permission from the police. It was granted and we moved to our new house.

This time there was no buggy and we lugged our belongings from one side of the village to the other. Although at that time Rubtsovsk was still small as far as its native population, housing, and facilities were concerned, it sprawled over a very large area and it took us well over an hour each way and several trips. I don't know how it was done, but even in that austere time we had accumulated more than our bags and hamper could hold—another pot or two, a sack of flour, a bag of potatoes—and some of it we carried wrapped in sheets on our backs.

The seven of us jammed into one of the rooms. This room was just barely large enough for two *nari* and not another stick of furniture. We *lived* on those two beds —ate, slept, rested, engaged in conversation, quarreled, and when I went back to school I would have to study there too. But we had a major preoccupation in that room—fighting bedbugs. Bedbugs crawled the beds, the walls, the ceiling, and the floor of that room, and no amount of kerosene seemed to help. True, the Siberian hut is noted for breeding bedbugs—possibly the manure has something to do with it—but that particular hut must surely have been an extreme case.

All things considered, including the combined smell of kerosene and manure, a trip to the other room to use the stove was a treat, even though our landladies made it clear that they wished this were not necessary. They also made it clear that they did not want the little boy to have anything to do with me. The only person who extracted a good morning or a good evening from them was Father and even he gave up after a while.

But one evening Father did not return from work.

"Perhaps the books did not balance," Mother said, "and he is looking for the mistake."

I went outside and peered down the darkening road. There were no street lights; one depended on the lights in the huts or the moon, when it was up, to light the streets. But there was not one shadow moving through that murkiness. It was bitter cold and I returned to the hut.

After a while, Grandmother said: "Such a big mistake, Raya?"

"A little mistake can take a long time," Mother answered shortly.

Then, much to my relief, Mother decided to bring Father some food. Who knew how long he might have to stay there working?

She came back with the food. Her voice was trembling, in spite of her effort to keep calm: the place was deserted!

"Mama . . ."

She put her finger to her lips and indicated that we

were not to add to Grandmother's alarm. "Raya . . . Raya . . ." Grandmother began.

"Perhaps a friend took him home for a bowl of good soup . . ."

I was finding Mother's unusual optimism more alarming than reassuring.

Even Anya didn't primp that night; instead, she told me my hair was a sight and she would brush it. But I was too restless and kept running to the door to look out.

The hours went by. The stars came out. And a full moon. But no Tata. That night I didn't pray; I issued an order.

Finally, we all undressed and crept under our covers. We played a game. We pretended that no, Father hadn't gone home with a friend, he had been called away on business, very important business. We called good night to each other and everyone pretended to be asleep.

I was awake most of the night listening and I imagine that the sounds I willed to be Father's footfall on the road were in reality the pounding of my heart.

The morning came and Father had not returned. Mother went to the bakery to say that she was sick and would have to see a doctor. She was given leave for the day and a pass to the doctor. She came straight home to join us in our vigil.

All day we waited, taking turns looking out the window. What are we *waiting* for? I wanted to ask. Why don't we *do* something? But there was something about Mother's stony face that made me keep my questions, and my tears, to myself.

The bleak northern afternoon was fading when I spotted a stooped figure approaching our hut. I nudged Mother. Neither one of us really wanted to look; this would be someone bringing bad news. The door opened and it was Tata. Barely recognizable. His eyes had sunken into a face as white as the Siberian snow, his hands were trembling violently.

"Tata—" I started to throw myself at him. "What happened?"

Mother grabbed me. "What difference does it make what happened? Tata is here, that's all that matters."

"Sugar . . . ?" Father asked faintly.

Yes, we had some. We hoarded sugar for emergencies, for the times when extreme fatigue or despair or the weakness of illness required energy.

Father took a teaspoon of sugar and a glass of water, his trembling hand spilling it. Then he lay down and closed his eyes.

"Everything is all right," he murmured. "I will tell you later—"

He fell asleep and slept for many hours, while we all huddled on the Kaftals' bed. That night, by silent consent, we did not use the sisters' stove; no one wanted to face their dour faces or the possibility of their questions (until now they had remained as taciturn as usual, saying nothing, asking nothing); besides, for once we were not hungry. We kept the lamp low, burning our precious oil, and watched over Father.

At last Father woke up and Mother gave him another teaspoon of sugar and some bread. His hands still trembled.

Then he began to talk. An N.K.V.D. agent, a member of the dreaded secret police, had come for him in the morning and taken him to their office. Did we know that they had separate offices, not at all connected with the local police? No, we didn't know it, but in asking the question, Father seemed to imply that this separateness added to the power and the terror of their secretiveness.

"The lights . . ." he shielded his eyes with his fluttering fingers, "such lights . . . they sat me in front of them . . . and they talked . . . and they talked . . . questions . . . questions . . . hours and hours . . . they took turns . . . they never stopped . . . I never dreamed the human voice could be such a weapon . . . on and on . . . twenty-four hours? . . . I don't know . . . maybe more . . . I lost time . . . I lost . . ." His voice trailed off.

"What?" Mother asked. "What did they want?"

"You won't believe it." He shook his head as if he too could not believe it. "They wanted me to be a spy——"

"A spy . . . ?"

Falling from our lips the word was like a hiss.

"They wanted me to spy on all the Polish people in the village and report on their activities. 'What activities?' I asked. 'What do you think we do besides try to keep body and soul together? Our activities? Are you mad?' "

"You said that, Samuel?" Mother asked, horrified.

"I said that. I told them that our activities are to feed our families, to keep warm, to keep from being caught in the storms outside. I talked that way, Raya. Me. I could hardly believe my own ears, that I had the courage to talk this way to secret police. I still can't believe that they didn't shoot me, that I am here——"

"Yes, yes, you are here, Tata, you are here——"

"I will take your word for it, lalinka——"

We waited for him to continue. At last he said: "I also cried. Like a baby. For the first time in years. It was after all the threats—deportation, God knows what. It was when they were bribing me. Food. A better house. Cigarettes. I put my head down on the table and I begged them to stop. No, I told them, I would not spy on my friends. I told them they could shoot me——"

I put my arms around Father. I was proud, very proud of my father. And I was still very frightened for him. Would they come back for Tata?

CHAPTER 10

A question like that in a place like that becomes a perpetual shadow.

But a breeze or two reminiscent of spring on its way, however agonizingly slowly, began to come up from the south and I was allowed to go back to school.

The children gathered round me: even in Siberia there was nothing like a broken limb or a prolonged illness to make a momentary hero or heroine of the most ignored child. What had I been sick with? typhus? flu? pneumonia? scarlet fever? they asked cheerfully and were quite disappointed that it had been only bronchitis, although they did seem moderately pleased that I had survived. Only Svetlana continued to act as if a fatal illness would have suited her better and she was most impatient with my inability to catch up with the work I had missed.

I was beginning to feel less of an outsider, almost —not quite—as if I belonged. I enjoyed the irony of the little capitalist joining the little comrades as we sang the "Internationale" in assembly ". . . arise ye prisoners of starvation, arise ye humble of the earth . . ." I sang as loudly and lustily as the rest . . . "'tis the final conflict . . . for the international Soviet shall be the human race . . ." and up went my fist along with the rest. There was a great deal of choral singing in the assembly, most of it unfortunately political rather than classical. But singing along with the others helped the feeling of belonging. However, among ourselves, away from assembly, we sang the songs that pleased us most, great favorites being Russian folk songs.

The news that an *American* movie was coming to Rubtsovsk sent the school into a dither. The Russian movies (including some of the great ones) were all right, but nothing was as exciting as an American movie. Everyone wanted to go. It was *the* topic: Are you going? Aren't you going? When are you going? Who are you going with?

Two girls invited me to go with them.

I was beside myself. An invitation in itself was something I longed to accept—any invitation would do—and I also longed to see a movie. And how much does it cost? I asked. Four rubles, I was told.

"Four rubles!" Mother exclaimed. "That's a lot of money."

My heart sank and I could feel an enormous wail coming up in me. I held it back and merely looked tragic. A family council was called. "Man cannot live by bread alone," my fun-loving grandmother said.

"That's the whole point," Mother agreed acidly. "Four rubles toward a piece of meat . . . ?"

"You call that *meat?*" Grandmother was getting cross.

Father, the great peacemaker, intervened. "The child must go to the movie."

"*Must?*" Mother asked, and even Grandmother looked surprised.

"*Must,*" Father repeated, and refused to amplify, leaving the strong impression that the fate of all Polish deportees was at stake. Behind their backs he winked at me.

The movie theater, which I now decided was a very pretty little white building, was behind the market place and close to a small park which, for some reason, was ignored by the children of Rubtsovsk. Possibly because it was the gathering place for the grownups. But tonight many children were streaking across it on their way to the movie.

The auditorium was jammed with squealing children; no teachers here, only ordinary grownups whose admonitions to quiet down didn't count.

The light dimmed (there was electricity here, of course, the first I had seen since I left Vilna) and everyone quieted down and waited attentively.

The movie was *Charlie's Aunt* with Jack Benny— with Russian subtitles—and we screamed with laughter. It was strange though to be sitting in this bare hall in Siberia watching an English classic that had been made in Hollywood. Walking home in the dark, surrounded by the huge steppe now broken by patterns in the slightly melting snow, it was Jack Benny, cavorting around in his ridiculous wig, who was most present, the scenes of Oxford that were most real.

That movie lasted us a long time; we hashed and re-hashed it until there was scarcely a reel that went unremarked. And it brought me just a bit closer to belonging, a condition I was beginning to hold more blissful than a full belly. A day that I was invited to play a game of dominoes or hopscotch I counted a big one, one that sent me home bursting to tell my grandmother about it.

But I had no best friend, no one to tell secrets to, no one to play games with. By all the rules and regulations, it should have been Svetlana who was my best friend. Svetlana did not see it that way.

At first, I thought it was because she was a snob. Her father was the director of the dairy farm and therefore a member of the managerial class. They lived in a clean little white house with *curtains* at the window and they had milk every day and eggs frequently. I went to her house to get my books, but I never was invited to stay. I had noticed that the children of the "big shots" tended to stick together and I thought that Svetlana was afraid to have a miserable little deportee as her best friend, that it would dethrone her as the queen bee.

But little by little, I saw that she was not a snob, that she was friendly enough with other children much less fortunate than herself. Why not me?

The answer to that was whispered into my ear as a secret I was to keep if I wished to live. The informer, another girl in my class, whispered that it was Svetlana who envied *me*—not my "fairy tale" past but, of all things, my braids, my less than shining-clean long braids. Since I did wish to live, I used all the will power I had to keep from telling Svetlana that to keep long braids even reasonably clean was a great chore. We almost never had soap, and hot water was a problem when so many people had to use the stove and when cinders were scarce too.

I kept the secret but I began my campaign to have my braids cut off. The direct approach didn't work.

"Please cut my braids off," I asked Mother.

Mother responded with a firm "No!" the kind from which there was no appeal.

Exactly what my braids represented to my mother then, I don't know. I continued to nag; she continued to stand firm. I scratched my head ostentatiously; I bit on my braids; I pretended that their odor was enormously offensive to me.

"You have *always* had long hair," Mother said.

"Everyone else has short hair."

"As good a reason as I have ever heard for having long hair."

"But—"

"But you are you and they are they."

"I don't want to be me, I want to be them. You don't understand."

Perhaps she didn't. But it must have hurt to contemplate even the possibility that her child might discard her own rich heritage for a toe hold in this land of exile, this thoroughly alien land.

"Esther!" There was both pain and shock in the exclamation.

I covered my ears. The battle between the generations was on.

"I'll cut it myself," I threatened, unusually rebellious for me. "And it will be a great mess—"

I burst into tears, tears of confusion and frustration as much as anything else. Didn't anyone care that I *needed* to belong, *needed* a best friend?

"We'll talk about it tomorrow," my mother said slowly.

The next evening Mother told me curtly that she was going to cut my hair, but it was because there was no soap and for no other reason, certainly not because I wanted to look like everyone else. Did I understand? Oh, yes, I assured Mother, beside myself with joy and secretly blessing the lack of soap.

Anya provided the scissors and everyone some advice. Not too short. . . a little shorter . . . watch her ear . . .

"So . . ." Mother put the scissors down. She looked as if she were about to weep as she gathered the shorn braids together.

"Let me see—"

Anya held the mirror up and my heart sank. I looked like something the cat dragged in.

"A little hot water and some brushing . . ." Grandmother said none too optimistically.

In the end it was my father who almost convinced me that I looked absolutely marvelous and I couldn't wait to go to school the next morning. The final judgment would be made by my classmates, in particular Svetlana.

It worked. I had performed the initiation rite. For better or worse, I had become one of them.

"Hey, stupid . . ." a boy called out as I missed a ball he threw my way.

I was beginning to be happy. One day I might even be lucky enough, when my clothes were completely in tatters, to wear clothes like theirs. One day if I was very lucky, I might even get a green quilted jacket, a *fufaika*.

On the way to Svetlana's house, I told her of this secret wish. For the first time, she asked me to stay. We ate sunflower seeds, spitting the shells out till our chins were bearded with them.

Now I had a best friend.

I thought I would die of happiness.

CHAPTER 11

The spring came, the rather thin spring of the Siberian steppe.

But it is impossible to have any thoughts of the thin Siberian spring without first recalling the thick mud. What with the spring rains and the thaw, the steppe became an ocean of mud and to walk through it was like walking through knee-deep molasses. If one was not lucky enough to own a pair of *sapogy*, the handsome knee-high leather boots that the well-to-do wore, if one had nothing but the same old pair of school oxfords, or even *pimy* boots, along with the energy needed to pull a foot up from the bottom of this mud, one also more often than not had to stop to hunt for the shoe left behind. Whatever one wore, the object developed a crust of mud that had to be broken off after each excursion. While I may have found some of this fun, my mother did not; her trips to and from the bakery in the mud required more energy than she had. She said that time and again, exhausted, she would stand still, with both legs buried in the mud, thinking that only a derrick would be able to hoist her out.

Mud or no mud, Siberia notwithstanding, with the spring I was gay. I had a friend to whisper and gossip with; I played tag and hopscotch—which a less muddy patch in the schoolyard permitted—and along with the other girls, I watched the boys' preoccupation with their pigeons. Raising pigeons was one of their favorite pastimes, and luring the birds away from each other apparently its major objective.

Svetlana and I studied together and complemented each other: she helped me with my Russian grammar and spelling, and I helped her with ideas for themes. Although I always enjoyed school, going to school in Siberia became for me a daily trip to paradise. The return trip to the hut was not. The last day of school for me was a sad day.

As soon as school was over, we began to work on our potato crop for the coming winter.

The government had allotted individual plots of land on the outskirts of the village, and one bought tiny potatoes to sow, with the expectation that they would produce a new crop.

This was not a foregone conclusion with that unyielding earth. Very early in the morning, we would go out with shovels and sacks of potatoes to fight, cajole, and work this land. Whatever was produced here would belong to us, which was worth remembering as our backs ached and our skin blistered in the sun. And what was produced, what little, *did* belong to us. There was no pilfering in the unprotected, unguarded potato plots. Considering the empty bellies, this degree of honesty was astonishing.

With summer upon us, the hut became unbearably stifling, the vermin unbearably populous, and all tempers reacted accordingly—our landladies', the little boy's, and ours. After all, ten human beings were inhabiting this wretched little oven.

Father decided to investigate the possibility of finding us new quarters.

On the north side of the village, there were some dilapidated and unoccupied huts. Unoccupied with reason: there was no heating of any kind, no floors, and no glass in the windows. But they were empty. Father went to the village housing chief and asked if we might enjoy the privilege of occupying one of these huts.

About this time, factories were beginning to be built in Rubtsovsk—among them a huge tractor factory—and with them came a large migration from European Russia of engineers, technicians of all sorts, and workers. In order to house these people, large new buildings were erected near the factories and alongside the huts. The district where they existed became known as the *novostroyka*, meaning new buildings. To me, these buildings were the ultimate in beauty and comfort. They were painted white and yellow and light green and there were floors in them and some apartments even had bath-rooms, but these were only for the chiefs of the facto-ries.

Miraculously, we were permitted to move into one of the empty huts and we were to be alone at last!

The Kaftals elected to stay on with the sisters. Inevi-tably, seven people who had been virtually bedfellows ended up getting on one another's nerves.

As for me, the wretched little hut became my dream house. Every day, after working in the potato patch, I went there and cleaned it as best I could. We also picked up manure, mixed it with clay, and either replaced some of the old square blocks in the walls or repaired others. Father got some whitewash at the construction job and we covered the walls with it. And someplace or other we found glass for the windows.

Before we could cover the floor with fresh clay, we had to dig a cold cellar. Since it would be impossible to keep the potatoes from freezing in an outdoor cellar, we dug one in the middle of our room. Father found some split logs lying around the *novostroyka* and cov-ered the hole with them. Since the rounded logs were also still covered with bark, they gave our floor an odd look, but no matter: we had our own home and our own stove, an outdoor summer one that Father had con-structed of bricks, where we could cook our own little flour cakes and our own soup without lining up to do so—and without any helpful and unhelpful, welcome and unwelcome, hints as to their preparation.

That spring Mother had learned that there was such a marvelous thing as a public bath, a *bania*, in the vil-lage, and to get there became her dearest wish. What if we did eat a little less for a week or two to save up for such a treat? Wouldn't it be heavenly to feel *clean* before we moved to our own home?

The *bania* was in a small building with two entrances, one for men and one for women. We found that Mother was not the only woman with a passion for cleanliness: the line was long; the wait would be a couple of hours at least. We waited.

There were two rooms in the *bania*; one had stone benches and faucets along the walls, the other was a steam room, a rather crude sauna where one used twigs in the Finnish fashion to clean oneself and stir up one's circulation.

We were assigned a cubbyhole for our clothes and, since we were to use the room with the faucets, we were given a basin and a piece of pumice. We filled our basins at a faucet, sat down on a stone bench and scrubbed away. The water was *hot*. Mother was entranced. Now we were quite ready to move.

Outside the hut, there was a small piece of land that no one seemed to be using. With our potatoes, and some tomato plants and corn seed given to us by Svetlana, we would turn it into a vegetable patch.

The plans Grandmother and I were making for this garden inevitably recalled Grandfather and our garden in Vilna. As her eyes filled with tears, Grandmother tested my memory. Did I remember what Grandfather had said about the irises? and the pansies? Did I remember the lilac tree?

Yes, I remembered everything. I remembered exactly where Grandfather had said to plant each flower. I remembered the prize of fifty groshes that each week was given to the child whose flowers looked best. Yes, I remembered.

"Good!" Grandmother raised her head; she was proud of me. I had passed the test. "And you will never forget?" No, I would never forget. "Good!" Now my memory was to be honored, she seemed to say; it was to become the archive of her beloved past.

Could we plant some flowers? I wanted to know. Grandmother was a realist who lived in the future as well as the past; no, we could not, we needed every inch for growing food.

In this world of scarcity, the acquisition of the most trivial or seemingly useless object was a topic for conversation. So Svetlana told me that her father had gotten a large quantity of hospital gauze. (How and why I did not know or care to ask.) She asked me if I wanted some. I assured her I did; I would use it for curtains.

"White hospital gauze for curtains, Esther?"

"You will see," I said mysteriously.

I began to save onion peelings and asked Svetlana to do the same. In school, we had learned that onion peelings when boiled in water exuded a yellow pigment which could be used as dye. Svetlana had either forgotten this or else had no need to remember such things. She wondered what I was up to, but I told her it was a secret.

When I had gathered a big pile of onion peel, I boiled it until the water was a pot of pale yellow dye. I dunked the gauze in this, let it stay for several hours, and to my delight it worked. The gauze was a now a pretty yellow. I stretched it out and dried it in the sun and then I made our curtains. There were no curtain rods to be had, so we tacked them on with little nails, and my pride in the result was very great. Everyone agreed that the curtains were very pretty and just what this hut needed.

The hut was heaven. We ate when we wanted to, slept when we wanted to, at night we would sit outside and gaze at the Siberian sky where there was always something to see; we would sit there quietly, quietly. Even Mother seemed to regain some of her old zest for life.

It was too good to be true to last.

One day the village housing chief came to our hut when I was alone and told me that the next day we were to have a tenant, whether we wanted one or not.

"Who is it going to be?" I asked.

"Vanya, the bum."

"Vanya, the bum . . . ?" I was horrified.

I had been taught never to call anyone names, but everyone called this one-legged man "Vanya the bum." He was the village beggar and people said he stole. Now this bum was going to live with us? In Vilna, there had been many beggars. Whenever I saw them, I was morbidly affected. Where did they eat? Did they ever bathe at all? And, most important, where did they go at night? Where did they sleep? Thinking about them, I used to shudder.

Now one was going to live with us.

When I gave the news to my parents, they were no less stunned than I was.

"Vanya, the bum . . . ?" Father asked.

I assured him that I had heard correctly.

Mother coughed. A signal to father that she disapproved of his language. Vanya was not to be called a bum. The lecture that followed seemed to me—and perhaps to Father too—untimely, like correcting the grammar of someone who is trying to tell you the house is on fire. The lecture continued: Vanya was not to be called Vanya either. He must have a proper name. We were to introduce ourselves as usual, etc. Perhaps this man has a *worthy* reason for begging? Don't you *agree*, Samuel?

Father not only agreed, but having been rebuked, went on to remind me that we must not judge people by their appearance, etc., etc.

Fidgeting from foot to foot, I listened to everything they had to say, but as far as I was concerned, Vanya the bum was coming to live with us and I was not only terrified but revolted.

Perhaps the village housing chief would have a change of heart, I thought to myself.

The next evening, Vanya the bum stood at our open door.

"May I come in?"

"Of course you may." Mother stood up.

"Good evening." Father went toward Vanya.

"Good . . . evening." Vanya's response was tentative.

Regardless of all these amenities, this tall, bone-thin specter in filthy clothes, with dark bushy hair and a matted beard, was still a bum to me. But I felt Mother's eyes on me.

"Good evening," I said, going forward but keeping my hands rigidly at my sides. "My name is Esther Rudomin. What's yours?"

"Vanya."

His deeply sunken eyes darted from Mother to Father and back to me.

"My name is Ivan Petrovich, my child," he amended, and there was a tiny spark in his eyes.

"Welcome to our house, Ivan Petrovich," my father said.

For the first time, Grandmother, who had been watching this scene more or less huddled in her bed, spoke up. "Welcome," she murmured.

"Thank you, thank you. Where may I put down my stick? And this bag?" The bag was a tattered dusty bundle.

No one had given this matter a thought.

In a tiny room with a hole in its center and three of its corners already occupied by beds, the obvious answer was the fourth corner. But the intention had been to build the winter stove in that corner.

"So we will make the stove smaller," Mother said, answering our unspoken words, and pointed to the corner. "Maybe we can get some wood for a *nari*, like ours."

"Oh, please—don't worry about me. I'll be very comfortable just as it is." He smiled a little sardonically. "I beg your pardon for this intrusion. Your privacy—"

I could see that my parents and my grandmother were as impressed as I was at his language and his accent: this was no illiterate.

Using his stick dexterously, he hobbled off to his corner on his one leg. There, he stretched out on the floor with his head on his bundle and said that he would rest.

It was an awkward moment. It was still early; what

were we to do now? Just sit and watch this stranger rest?

"Please," he said with his eyes closed, "the child can sing and play and do anything she likes. When I am tired, I sleep and when I sleep, I sleep the sleep of the dead."

"Thank you," I said.

And I meant it. Living with a bum was going to be more agreeable than living with our former landladies, who were forever hushing me and the little boy.

The transformation from village bum to Ivan Petrovich did not take place overnight—either in my mind or in reality. At first he remained a shadowy figure from the dark world of the homeless, the friendless, the outcast. He left very early each morning and when he came home at night, he went directly to his corner—not that there was anyplace else to go. He talked very little, munched on bits of food he had picked up, and went to sleep. But before he ate, he always offered me anything he had brought—a fresh carrot, perhaps, or a beet. My parents always offered food in return, but he always refused. I, on the other hand, used to accept a bit of carrot or beet because I didn't want to hurt his feelings. Recently, Mother had amended her view of the etiquette for accepting precious food: When some was offered, you took a tiny bit if you thought they did not have enough, but that you took; it was only polite to do so.

After a few weeks had gone by, the transformation began: he started to eat with us, sharing whatever he had brought. If we cooked potatoes, we added his carrot to it and called it a vegetable stew. If it was a white beet, we boiled it until we could spread it on bread instead of jam.

Then he began to talk. Ivan Petrovich was a shoemaker from the Ukraine, a man who knew his craft and who had read many books: But once he had talked too much or too carelessly or had been misunderstood. He never did know why he had been sent to prison in Siberia; such a piece of information had been considered superfluous. And when he had been released, he had only one leg left and made his way from village to village begging.

Soon he began to wash himself, which pleased us more than it is polite to say. And to comb his beard. And to carry himself with dignity. He became Ivan Petrovich—for the time being at least.

When he first came to our house, we were the object of much curiosity: What is it like to have a bum in your house? Does he steal? How do you talk to a bum? How does he talk to you? Doesn't it make you shudder?

But as Ivan Petrovich came to regard himself differently, so did the villagers: he became much less a bum and much more just another human being cast off on the great Siberian steppe.

One day he disappeared. He left as usual early one morning and that was the last that any of us ever saw of Ivan Petrovich, formerly known as Vanya the bum.

CHAPTER 12

The second summer in Siberia was hot and dry, scorching the potato patch to fruitlessness. We tried to save the little patch of corn and tomatoes next to our hut with water lugged all the way from the river. We prayed for rain, but that was a summer of severe drought.

It was also a summer of typhus. Father managed to get fly paper which he hung about our hut and which we were always ducking; every drop of water we used was boiled. I knew that people were dying by droves. I was terrified.

And it was also the summer I saw Deanna Durbin in

100 Men and a Girl four times at the village movie house. In the annals of movie fanatics, this would not rate me a mention, but in order to get the sixteen rubles needed our menu became more austere than ever. Whatever my parents thought of my self-indulgence, they never said a word; once again they must have realized how great this other hunger was.

That summer, Deanna Durbin was our superheroine. Svetlana and the other girls and I talked about her by the hour. We sang her songs and we talked about her smile, her walk, her hair-do. But mainly we talked about her clothes; when the war was over, we would all dress like Deanna Durbin. How this was to be accomplished in Rubtsovsk was no concern of ours; true, there had been a scarcity of clothing even before the war, *but* . . . We dreamed on and on and sang Miss Durbin's songs, and when at last we tired of those, Svetlana, who played the balalaika and had a lovely voice, sang Russian songs. Soon I learned them too, and she and I would harmonize for hours on end.

On Sundays, throughout the year, whenever the weather permitted—and sometimes when it didn't—all of us children had an odd duty to perform. We gathered at a construction job—it didn't seem to matter which one—and hauled bricks back and forth in wheel barrows, dumping them down and picking them up. The practical reason was obscure. As far as we could make out, this activity was an exercise in patriotism— we were doing our bit for the war effort.

During the summer, we children also helped out at the nearby collective farms, weeding potato patches and cornfields and doing other odd jobs. Part of every week was spent this way. The sun blazed down on us, the work was hard, we all complained, and we all rather enjoyed it too. We were together.

September came and there was momentary relief from extreme heat and extreme cold; there was only the wind to contend with. We dug our potato patch and our harvest was frightfully poor. There were just a few pails of small green potatoes. Our corn was good, but sparse. And the tomatoes we had eaten during the summer. The long winter ahead was going to be a very hungry one and we did not discuss the matter of survival. We prayed.

One day the postman came to our house. In those days in Rubtsovsk, his sack would not be a heavy one; what with the war, the huge displacement of people with their whereabouts a mystery, and the remoteness of the village, no one received much mail. As the postman walked the village in his nondescript uniform, whenever he stopped at a hut, the people who inhabited it became objects of curiosity: Who had received a letter? from whom? about what?

As for us, we had received exactly one letter since we had come to Siberia. This was from my Uncle Ben in America, to whom my mother had written on the off-chance that somehow, sometime it would reach him. His letter had been short and kind and he had enclosed a fifty-dollar bill, which Father exchanged at the local bank for two hundred and fifty rubles. But this money could not be used at the state stores. The only place it could be used was on the free market, where these two hundred and fifty rubles bought us only one-quarter pound of butter, two pails of potatoes, and a sack of flour. Mother thanked my uncle and told him please not to send us any more money as it was practically worthless here, whereas she knew that in America fifty dollars could still go a long way.

This second letter was addressed to Father and was in a long white envelope. I examined it closely, as if it were something from another civilization. I felt an ill wind blow through the hut.

My anxiety, and my curiosity too, increased as I waited for Father to come home and open his letter; in fact, I came close to opening it myself once or twice.

"A letter for *me?*" Father too reacted with astonishment.

He opened it and took out a long piece of paper. I watched his face as he read: it had gone white and once again he looked the way he had the morning we were deported—old and defeated.

"What is it, Tata, what is it?" I cried out, terrified.

Still reading and rereading the letter, Father sat down on his bed.

He could not bear to tell me what was in the letter and with a futile effort at reassuring me, he murmured absurd phrases . . . it's nothing, nothing . . . everything will be all right. . . .

I finally extracted the terrible truth: Father was ordered to go near the front lines to work in a labor brigade. *Front lines!* Suddenly, this most gigantic of all wars with its bombings and battles and wounded and dead, this war that, in spite of our exile—or because of it—had until this moment seemed unreal, was now at our doorstep. True, even in Rubtsovsk, even I had heard of the ferocious battle that was going on between the

Russian and the German armies with the Germans pushing the Russians back to the Volga. But we saw no newspapers, seldom heard the radio. And now the war had exploded right here in this hut.

"Lalinka!" Father put his hand out toward me.

My face must have expressed my total anguish.

"No!"

"Lalinka, we must be brave. Come here——"

"No! I don't want to be brave. I'm sick and tired of being brave. Tata, *please* don't go, *please*, Tata . . ."

"You have grown up so much, my lalinka, you cook and you clean and you market, now will you grow up just a little bit more? A little bit? Enough to help your mother and grandmother through this?"

"But we are all alone here in Siberia, Tata. And Grandfather . . ."

"Shh! Where is your grandmother? Any second, she may come in. . . ."

He knew where she was. We all pretended that Grandmother no longer went out to the fields to weep alone for Grandfather. Now would it be for Tata too?

I ran to him and buried my face in his shoulder. He rocked me back and forth without saying a word.

Mother wept. Tears did not come easily to my mother and when she wept upon hearing this news, my worst fears were confirmed: for us, this news was tragic.

Now it was my turn. I tried to comfort Mother. I went over to her; she was sitting on the bed weeping and I put her head on my shoulder and stroked her hair. I told her that everything was going to be all right, that Father would not be gone long, that we would write to Father often and that he would write to us. I was playing at being grown-up, as if I were murmuring to a doll.

Mother raised her head and looked at me, and Father came over and kissed her on the cheek.

"Don't worry, Raya," he said. "I will be all right and you will be all right. You are strong, Raya, strong. You will take care of our child. And of yourself. And my mother . . . You will see that she is all right also . . ."

Mother nodded.

We sat on the bed in a silent huddle, exhausted by the emotion both expressed and unexpressed.

Grandmother came in and found us that way. She took the news as if there were no despair, no human degradation, no tragedy, personal or otherwise, that was beyond her ability to comprehend, to cope with. Beyond any question she had wept herself out in the fields that afternoon.

Looking at me, she said; "All of this is not for children."

The next day Father went to the authorities to get further instructions. They told him that he would be sent to a work brigade on the front lines. However, first he would join a large group being trained in a big town in Siberia.

Now Father the optimist took over: by the time he got to the front lines the war would be over; he would go directly from the front lines to Poland where he would send for us.

Mother held her tongue but she looked at him as if he had taken leave of his senses.

The day before Father left, Mother stayed home from her job. In the early morning they went off together to our potato patch to see if by any miracle there were any new potatoes or any that had been overlooked. It was a long walk to the patch and Mother, who had been suffering from sciatica, developed such a severe attack that she was unable to walk home and they slept on the earth beside the patch that night.

Where husbands and fathers going off to war in other parts of the world might spend some of their last hours at home going over their affairs with their wives, deportees in Siberia had only one affair to discuss—food. In our case, the matter of food was extremely serious. There was scarcely enough in our cellar to last two months, let alone the whole winter.

But the emptiness of our bellies would still be nothing compared to the emptiness of our hut without Father. The day Father left was the worst day of my whole life. I spent it weeping. I lay on my bed and wept incessantly. Not even Siberia had been able to extinguish my father's love of life—his charm and his gaiety. In Siberia, I had warmed myself at this bright light time and time again.

Mother saw Father off alone, without Grandmother or me. Grandmother went off to the fields and I stayed in the hut, still weeping.

CHAPTER 13

After Father left, life in the hut was indeed as desolate as we had thought it would be. Poor Mother, who way back there in that other time, that other world, had once been quick to laugh, to regard life with a sense of humor, even to relish its absurdity, tried to recall it for our benefit, Grandmother's and mine, tried to stand in for Father, but she was too tired, too worried about food and how we were going to heat our hut. As the autumn winds blew colder and colder, the woodpile appeared to shrink before our eyes. Where would we get the rubles for wood? How would we cut it up? In order to stretch the supply of wood, we also burned dry manure, which did not smell as awful as one might imagine.

There was this to be said about problems in Siberia: *they* were never in short supply, nor were they ever unique. At school I heard some of the children talking about the scarcity of fuel, how they would freeze to death except for . . .

"Except for what?" I asked, coming up to them.

They made a big to-do about looking around slyly and closing ranks before whispering to me that if I joined them that night I would find out.

"But can we trust her?" one of them inquired, looking me up and down.

Honor coming before prudence, I indignantly assured them I certainly was to be trusted before asking the question: with what?

Thus it was that I found myself on a moonless night part of a small band of children, each equipped with a burlap bag, stealing little pieces of coal that had dropped onto the railroad tracks. The other children seemed to be hardened criminals, even regarding this as a game, but if I had been robbing a bank I could not have felt more guilty or more frightened. With every sound I heard in the darkness, I felt the brutal arm of the law thrashing my fragile back. *Stealing in Siberia?* If Siberia was the place thieves were exiled to, was there an even worse place for Siberian thieves? And what about God? What would He do to me for breaking the commandment?

But I kept right on filling up the bag.

However, when our leader—a twelve-year-old boy with all the attributes of a boy scout—passed the word that we were to stop, my relief was enormous. But short-lived. We had only stopped stealing coal in order to leave room for stealing *struchki*. *Struchki* were wood shavings which we would steal from the lumberyard.

"Oh, thank you very much but the coal will do nicely," I said, preparing to part company with my accomplices.

"Oh, stop being such a coward. Come along." Creeping home through the dark village with my bag full of coal and *struchki*, I was still more concerned with the punishment than the crime. But I could also already feel my toes warming before the fires this haul would make.

When Mother and Grandmother asked me where I had got the coal and *struchki*, I said: "Don't ask."

They exchanged glances and a knowing smile, these two women whose code did not permit them to take so much as a crumb belonging to someone else. In Vilna, that is.

I soon discovered that not only bands of children but grownups, too, combed the tracks and yards for coal and *struchki* and I joined them time and time again. But I never enjoyed it; I always felt both guilty and scared.

Moreover, stealing was not really to the taste of one who still clings to pride. Mother reported that someone said that I walked around the village holding my head up high, as if I were the child of one of the chiefs, not like a poor little deportee at all. So? I reminded Mother that when she had to walk barefoot through the village she hid herself when she saw someone she knew coming toward her. She shrugged. "So we are both proud—for the time being—"

During those first weeks after Father went away, nothing distracted me from my sense of loss—not even stealing. Every day I waited for a letter in vain; always inside me the same question: Will I ever see my father again?

Mother came home one night looking even more haggard and worried than usual. Half a dozen people at work had been reported ill with what appeared to be ordinary grippe. Three of them were dead. Dead in three days. "Why do you come home with such terrible stories?" Grandmother wanted to know, glancing my way out of the corner of her eye.

"Because I don't want Esther—or you either—to die of the flu!" Mother retorted. Mother went on to tell us that we were in the midst of a severe epidemic, that people were dying like flies, and that we were to take every possible precaution. Why, she wanted to know, hadn't I been told about this at school? Been warned? The very next morning we learned that one child had lost both parents within twenty-four hours of each other.

One does not become immune to terror. Now I became terrified that I might lose either Mother or Grandmother or both of them. They did not get it, but I did. When Mother saw that I was feverish—and like most mothers she knew the degree without the aid of a thermometer—she became as close to hysterical as I was ever to see her. The trembling, white-faced, wild-eyed, silent kind of hysteria. Fortunately, mine turned out not to be a dangerous case. The doctor came to see me once and we were shocked to see how tired and drawn she looked. The story of the difficulties of handling an epidemic of this magnitude without enough doctors or medicine was written on her face. However, she had been promised that with the influx of workers, she would soon have an infirmary that was better equipped and possibly another doctor or two. Soon? Perhaps not soon enough.

Although I was not seriously ill, I still had to stay in bed for several weeks. And lying in bed, I listened and listened for the postman. He never came.

Life seemed utterly miserable and cheerless and I did little to conceal this view from Mother. One night she stared at me for a long time, as if to say, What am I going to do with this poor woebegone creature? Suddenly she decided what to do: "You're going to have a birthday party, a real birthday party!"

Ah, I thought, now Mama has gone crazy. A birthday party in Siberia? Here in this hut? I had almost forgotten that there were such days as birthdays.

My birthday comes late in October on the same day as my parents' wedding anniversary. At home it had always been a particularly gay occasion. Preparing for it was part of the excitement and fun. For weeks, Mother and the cook baked cakes and cookies and made candy, filling the house with delicious smells of sugar and spices. And Miss Rachel and I made accordion-pleated clowns' ruffs and hats out of gold paper; we cut and pasted sheets of tinted papers into all manner of decorations—place cards, little baskets for nuts and candies, flowers, what have you—each year making them a little more elaborate than the year before as my fingers became more deft. And every birthday, I was the Queen and my cousin Salik, whose birthday was the same day, was the King. As many as fifty children came to our party and the high spot of the afternoon was always the Charlie Chaplin movies Father would have rented along with a projector.

In the evening, Father and Mother had their party and, having been tucked into bed with the special kisses parents give children on their birthdays, I would fall asleep to the sound of their laughter, secure in the knowledge that mine was the best of all possible worlds.

My twelfth birthday was celebrated in a dung hut in Siberia.

Quite recklessly, Mother used up almost all the potatoes we had in the cellar (potatoes that we had expected to last at least another month), to make an enormous pot of potato goulash.

Mrs. Kaftal, Karl, and Anya came and so did Mrs. Marshak and Boris. And there were one or two other people Mother had met at the *baracholka* and several friends who were from the Polish deportee community.

They came with gifts: an apple, a piece of meat, a sweet beet, and a large bag of sunflower seeds; lovely gifts, deeply appreciated.

Short of fuel, we sat with our coats on, sat on the beds. Short of bowls and spoons, we took turns eating the goulash. They sang a birthday greeting to me and the grownups gossiped, while I listened and Boris fell asleep.

Everyone said it was a wonderful party, and it was.

When it was over, Mother and Grandmother and I rehashed it the way people always do after a party. "Didn't Anya look pretty?" "I think they really enjoyed the goulash." "A trifle salty perhaps . . ."

But later we were very quiet. Mother lay on her bed with her eyes closed, but she wasn't asleep. Grandmother and I had each given her a kiss, wishing her well on her wedding anniversary.

Where was Tata? Where were the rest of our family? If only we were all together here in Siberia. God alone knew what was happening to them in German-occupied territory, I had heard it whispered. At least we were alive.

When Mother opened her eyes, as if she had read my thoughts, she said: "We laughed today. We were happy over an apple and a piece of meat . . . Life goes on. Someday it will be better. It will, Esther, it will."

CHAPTER 14

Father had disappeared into an unknowable place with a strange address. For some reason—perhaps the same reason that makes one want to see the ship, the plane, or the train come in with the returning traveler one loves—I had so wanted to see the postman bring the first letter from Tata, watch him stop at our house for once, be the one to receive the letter into my own hands.

This was not to be. The letter arrived when we were all out and the postman unceremoniously dropped it on the ground.

The letter was one meant for the censor's eyes as well as ours. It told us very little about Father, nothing about where he was or what he was doing except that he was not yet near the front. In his beautiful script, he assured us that everything was going to turn out all right, that if a new Deanna Durbin movie came to the village, lalinka was to memorize all the songs and sing them to him when he came home, that we were not to worry, not to worry. . . . Father was trying to be gay and optimistic.

It was many weeks before we heard from him again.

I wanted to tear a page out of an old schoolbook that I was now using to do my homework in—writing between the printed lines as I would in newspapers too—and write to Father immediately, but Mother wisely reminded me of my teacher's forbidding disposition, and Grandmother thought it wasn't seemly for Father to receive a letter from home on raggedy paper. But one couldn't buy any paper anyplace, even if one had the rubles, so we ended up writing to Father between the lines of some old newspaper. We wrote in script as tiny as we could make it.

Mother and Grandmother picked up every scrap of war news they could get hold of, mostly on the *baracholka*. Our greatest wish was that the war would end before Father was sent close to the front. But the news from the front was very bad. Town after town in European Russia was being besieged by the Germans and the stories of their atrocities filtered down to our village.

Mother and Grandmother no longer attempted to hide from me their deep concern about our family. We prayed for their well-being. But time and time again, Mother wished aloud—and countless times she must have done so silently—that she had told the Russian soldiers that morning in Vilna that the man who had knocked on the door was her brother. If she had, he would have been here now, safe, with us, she would say in anguish. Mother had begun at about this time, she told us later, to have her dreadful foreboding about the fate of my aunts and uncles and of my cousins too, a foreboding that made her cry out in her sleep and that she could not tolerate when awake.

The potatoes in our cellar were down to one week's supply and we had only one thirty-ruble note to carry us through the whole month.

The monthly five rubles was due for my school lunch, which consisted of a slice of bread and a piece of cheese if and when it was available, and since there was no other way, Mother had to give me the thirty-ruble note to take with me. This she did, warning me to watch it for dear life—scarcely an exaggeration—and begging me to count the change carefully (for me, two and two did not always readily add up to four). "Remember," she reminded me needlessly, "that this money is all we have for the rest of the month." Then, as if it would prod me to heed her warnings, she said that along with our ration of bread, there might even be some sugar given out this time.

It was bait that made my mouth water. My idea of heaven at that time was to have all the bread in the world that I could eat and all the sugar that I could pile into my mouth. Fresh bread—preferably white—and sugar had become more appealing to me than cakes and cookies and chocolate.

I went off to school that morning clutching the thirty-ruble note in my hand, just as Mother had told me to do—for dear life. It only left my hand when I had to write and read; then it went into my pocket.

When the time came for us to line up for lunch, I

reached down into my pocket for the money. There was an emptiness there that I felt in the pit of my empty belly.

I began to search. My desk. My books. Other people's desks. Their books. I crawled on my hands and knees all over the classroom. This cannot be, I assured myself, I will find the money, we will not starve. I went up to everyone in school, including the teachers, and asked them if they had seen a thirty-ruble note.

No one had seen it. The money was gone and with it our bread for the month.

I not only felt sick with despair, but also frightened. Mother didn't get angry with me often, but when she did, it was overwhelming. All of my past offenses dwindled to minor infractions compared to losing this money. I simply did not want to go back to the hut and stalled as long as I could. I walked around the village trying to figure out some way of replacing the money . . . or getting the bread. I had some quite desperate fantasies. Having already discovered that I was not much good as a thief, I wondered whether I would fare any better as a beggar. Finally, there was no escape: I had to go home.

It was very late and Mother was full of concern. Why was I so late? Had anything happened to me?

"I won't say. You can be as angry with me as you wish. I don't know what to say. And I don't know what happened. I don't. I don't." My voice began to quaver and my teeth to chatter. I didn't cry; I just shivered from head to foot. It was not calculated; it was unavoidable.

In a second both Mother and Grandmother were

fussing over me: What in God's name was the trouble? Was I sick? Surely nothing could have happened that was terrible enough to make me act this way?

"But it did!" I cried out. "It did! The thirty rubles—they're gone—"

I had a rather spectacular fit of hysterics, weeping and gasping for breath.

The two women stood absolutely still for a minute or two, trying to absorb this latest misfortune.

The next thing I knew I was in Mother's arms and she was stroking my hair. "Oh, my darling, we have lost so much more in our lives than this thirty-ruble note. You must stop your crying and your shivering. Everything will be all right."

Grandmother had gone to the pot of very watery soup that was our supper for that night.

"A nice cup of soup, Esther . . ."

"No, no. I can't eat. Now or ever. There will be nothing to eat the rest of this month. . . ."

I was on the verge of starting my hysterics all over again.

And Mother started talking—to me, to Grandmother, and to herself I am sure. Standing in for Father, she was assuring us that everything was going to be all right: we would not starve, we had friends, didn't we? (Grandmother and I nodded, although we knew that for Mother to ask anyone for a crust of bread was unthinkable.) We would find something to sell.

She stopped talking.

Selling the food one got at the state store on the free market was illegal and punishable to an uncomfortable degree, rumor had it. When she picked up the piece of bread we had left, I knew what was going through her mind.

"I'll do it, Mama."

"No, not you—"

We argued back and forth and, frightened to death about it as she was, and indeed as I was too, it was settled that I would try to sell the bread the next day.

"Before Tata left, he told us we were strong women and that we would get on well without him," Mother said. "And so we will." She put her hand on my head. "But you will be very very careful, Esther, won't you?"

The next day after school I went to the free market with our piece of bread. I carried it under my coat, as surreptitiously as the old women with the bread they wished to have blessed. I was becoming skilled in the ways of deception and no one caught me. I sold the piece of bread for twenty rubles, which reduced our loss to ten rubles.

Whether inspired by Mother's including me among the strong women who would get on well, or frightened by the prospect of starvation, that was the day that I decided that somehow or other I too must earn some rubles.

After supper, I waited for Grandmother to finish pushing back her cuticles—a process I thought would never end—and lie down on the mattress of straw, which even her tiny frail body had begun to make a bed of lumps. When I heard the pathetic little wheezes that accompanied her troubled sleep, I signaled to Mother that I wanted to talk to her. As I talked of my intention to become a breadwinner, I watched Mother's still beautiful but ravaged face for praise that surely was due me for being such an enterprising person. But Mother's face remained strangely opaque.

"What's the matter?" I asked, considerably deflated.

Then, as if she were pleading my case before some unearthly court, she murmured: "She is only twelve years old, she helps keep house like a little old woman, she studies like a Talmudic scholar, she carries bricks back and forth—" She caught her breath. "No. Enough is already too much. Esther, there is nothing more you can do that I will permit you to do. Just do well at school, that's all I ask. The way things are, you will need every drop of education you can get. For the rest —you leave the rubles to me."

"But, Mama——"

"Esther! Please not tonight. Tonight I don't have the strength for your 'buts.' "

"But I can knit and I can embroider, can't I? You and Miss Rachel taught me how, didn't you?"

Mother's lips twisted. "But of course. All the gentle arts——"

"Well, I will use them right here to make some money."

Mother was absolutely certain that rough as life was, every single woman in Rubtsovsk knew how to knit just as well as I did.

"But we can ask around, can't we? You ask your friends and I'll ask my friends. We'll spread the word."

For me, spreading the word meant that I had to admit to my friends that I needed work badly, that we really did not have enough food to see us through the winter. As my hunger grew, my pride shrank and so did my price—although I apparently still kept my head up as high as I could get it. I reduced it from "some" rubles to a little bit of milk or a cup of flour or some potatoes. Still there were no customers. Mother was right; everyone in Rubtsovsk did know how to knit and didn't need me.

I had given up all hope when a young woman came to our hut late one afternoon. She had some old white wool: would I knit a sweater for her little girl?

Would I? Presented at last with a real live customer, I was so flustered that I could barely talk.

"Don't *you* know how to knit?" I asked the lady, more incredulous than businesslike.

"Yes," she said.

"Then—?"

She held out her right arm and to my horror I saw that most of her hand was gone. I looked away quickly. Mother, who thought of everything, had not thought of this.

The woman showed me the wool—barely enough for a sweater for a midget—and said the sweater was to be a surprise for her little girl, who was not well.

"I cannot pay you much—"

A dreadful thought buzzed around me: Ought I to take anything at all from a poor crippled woman?

"—but I have a cow. Would one liter of milk and maybe a pail of potatoes be enough?"

Milk? And potatoes? The buzzing stopped. I was thrilled.

"Could you possibly have it ready for the New Year?"

Oh, yes, I assured the lady, although how this was to be done with everything else I had to do, I did not know.

"My little girl will be so happy," the lady said.

That makes two little girls, I thought.

Mother was amazed and, it turned out, delighted. She showed me how to start the sweater, but I had to rip it out a million times before I really got going. I worked on it whenever I had a spare minute and far into every night. The light in our hut was very poor. We had one we kept the wick down as low as possible. Moreover, the lamp had to rest on the one and only table, which was not close enough to the stove to keep my fingers warm. In order for them to be nimble enough to knit, I had constantly to jump up to warm them at the stove. But at last the sweater was finished and neatly pressed with an iron borrowed from Anya, who had surely gone hungry to acquire one.

My customer greeted me warmly and said I must meet her little girl. Having been told only that her child was "not well," I was not prepared for the pinched and white-faced little creature who sat up in bed to stare at me in a most peculiar way, with her little eyes squinting and her head twisting this way and that.

After a few stilted words—the little girl spoke in a wee little voice—the mother ushered me out. "My little girl is going blind and there's nothing we can do about it. I am glad you did such a good job on the sweater. Whenever she wears it, it will make her happy."

She gave me the milk and potatoes and I walked home filled with pride.

That night, as we feasted on the milk and potatoes, I saw a bright future with customers lining up in front of our hut to offer me work.

"She is her father's daughter, always the optimist," Mother said, shaking her head.

"And a good thing it is," Grandmother retorted. "If she had not been such an optimist, would we be drinking this milk and eating these potatoes?"

Mother did not answer, but I could tell that she was wondering how many crippled women there could be in one little village.

Indeed, it was a long time before I saw another customer, and since the nights had become too cold for stealing, fuel had become a most serious problem.

Mother and I kept staring at the few sticks of wood that were left as if we thought that our eyes would bewitch them into multiplying.

"What are we going to do, Mama?"

For a long time, she didn't answer. Then she jumped up and studied the logs covering our cellar.

"These are longer than they need be. We'll saw off the ends, that's what we'll do."

"But we're not strong enough——"

"Of course we are. All we need is a saw."

I started to giggle.

"What's so funny?"

"I don't know. Sawing up your house to heat it seems funny to me."

Mother began to laugh too.

"Tata would think we were crazy," I said.

"No, he wouldn't. He would be proud. . . ."

I borrowed a saw from Svetlana, whose house seemed not only like a horn of plenty but a bazaar compared to ours.

Huffing and puffing and unimaginably awkward,

Mother and I went to work with the saw. Watching us, Grandmother let out little shrieks: "Watch your foot!" "Your hand!" "Oh, my God!" "Stop! It's better to freeze to death than—"

It was a great deal of work and the return was barely enough to warm the hut for a week.

Mother stretched out on her bed, her body heavy with aching muscles and depressed spirits. "Perhaps—perhaps we should ask Uncle Yozia if he knows where we can get some wood," she said.

Uncle Yozia and his wife, Zaya, were new friends whom mother had met at the *baracholka*. He was an engineer and she was a piano teacher and they had come to Siberia from Kharkov when the tractor factory was built a year or two earlier. I fell in love with them at first sight.

Uncle Yozia had the most beautiful hands I have ever seen on a man. In our family, where the snobbism was to have been a scholar or a poet, I had watched adult eyes travel instinctively to a man's hands. That a scoundrel might also have the hands of an artist simply didn't occur to me. But whatever sensibilities those hands bespoke was more than confirmed in his funny gentle face, a face that reflected serenity, along with a half smile—enhanced by a slight cast in one eye—that gave him the air of a man with a joke tucked up his sleeve.

And Zaya. Zaya's round, cheerful face with sparkling green eyes was a magic lantern that transformed a dark smelly hut into a sunlit place.

Yes, I loved them very much.

That they had so warmly befriended some Polish deportees said something else about them too. For

Yozia and Zaya, although they were Jews, belonged to another social set in the village. There were "crowds," groups of people who associated only with each other and rarely mingled with anyone else. Having come with the tractor factory from European Russia, they belonged to the elite. They lived in one of the "beautiful" white houses where they had a two-room apartment and a bathroom!

There was much that they offered us, that they would have been more than happy to give us—some food, a real bath—but Mother always politely refused. Fenced in by her pride, Mother was a difficult woman to help. "Why?" I would ask, angry and bewildered, when she would refuse a gift of luscious piece of meat for instance.

"We do not want our friendship to be a burden to them."

But, I thought, if you are supposed to be generous, who are you supposed to be generous to? Only those who don't need it? It was very confusing.

There was only one thing that Mother had not been able to resist: Zaya, who had given up trying to share anything with Mother, had dropped a cake of soap on our table with feigned casualness just as she was about to leave. Mother's reaction was instantaneous and extreme: she grabbed the soap as if it were going to change the course of our life and her eyes glistened with tears as she clutched it to her bosom. "Soap!"

Uncle Yozia threw his head back and laughed. "It's as they say, there is no tyrant like a woman whose enemy is a speck of dirt."

"You can laugh," Mother said, beginning to laugh herself, "but after a nice bath and fresh clothes, one can face anything better—even the gallows."

With Mother restricting its use as if she were a miser, that evening she, Grandmother, and I felt the first soapy water touch our skin since that June morning ages ago! Soap had it all over clay and pumice too. We carried on and cooed with delight.

However, that cake of soap was the only thing Mother had accepted from Zaya and Uncle Yozia. When she considered asking Uncle Yozia about wood (*about*, not *for*), admitting that we were in great need, I knew she was desperate.

"And shouldn't we ask him to tell his friends about my knitting?" I asked, trying to take advantage of Mother's weak moment.

"No!" she said sharply. "He wouldn't like it. He thinks you do too much already. He's worried about you. He doesn't think you look well. I don't want to tell him you would take in knitting. That would make him feel sorry for us. We do not want their pity, Esther. Only their friendship—"

"But, Mama——"

"God in heaven, what 'but' have we got now?"

"But Mama—asking for work is not asking for pity. You said so yourself, your very own self. Isn't work something to be proud of?"

"You and your 'but.'" Mother smiled. "Only this time, you happen to be right. But——"

I laughed. "Mama, you have some 'buts' too."

"But let's wait," Mother said, a little sheepishly.

"Let's not ask Uncle Yozia about the knitting for a few days. Let's—let's— Esther, what about that handsome lady we see around the village——"

"The one you say looks like Anna Karenina?"

"Yes. What about telling her that you knit?"

I looked at Mother in utter amazement.

"But, Mother—she's a complete stranger! I don't understand you. . . ."

Mother was silent.

Then, "I don't understand myself. Only—I think it's precisely because she is a stranger, a complete stranger, living in a strange world . . ."

CHAPTER 15

We learned that her name was Marya Nikolayevna, that she had escaped from the German invasion of Leningrad, and that her husband was a high officer in the army. (The *baracholka* had become our newspaper, giving us the latest news from the front and tidbits of gossip.)

On a wintry Sunday, with the huge sky heavy with clouds warning that once again a storm was on the way, the people on the *baracholka* were trading with the special desperation an impending storm always bred. And yet, storm or no storm, all heads turned as Marya

Nikolayevna made her appearance. Wearing a sealskin coat and diamond earrings, she strolled around the *baracholka* like royalty visiting a charity bazaar.

That day I had gone to the *baracholka* for the sole purpose of talking to Marya Nikolayevna. I had nothing to sell and no rubles to spend. It was to be my third and last attempt to open my mouth in this lady's presence. That day I looked up at the clouds, thought of the storm to come, our bare larder, and our short supply of wood, and said to myself that it was now or never: today, I would ask this lady if I could do some knitting for her.

I pushed my way through the shivering, shabbily dressed crowd to the lady in the sealskin coat. Close up, she was even more beautiful than I had thought. Her skin had remained fair and incredibly luminous, as if even the ferocious climate, so cruel to other women, had been subdued by this royal creature.

Hoping it would take forever, I stood aside and waited for her to finish her inspection of a beaten-up teapot. (What, I wondered, did this great lady want with such an object? I had forgotten for a second that in Siberia all sorts of things were in short supply, even for the very rich.) When Marya Nikolayevna concluded that this pot was not for her, after turning it every which way, I forced myself to go up to her.

"My name is Esther Rudomin—" I began, my name sounding unfamiliar to me.

The icy wind that was blowing up didn't help; as I stood there shivering in my skimpy threadbare little coat, lifting my face to talk to the lady who was pulling her seal coat closer around her, it blew my words away so that I ended up having to shout that I was looking for work. But this wind carried Marya Nikolayevna's words down to me without any effort on her part at all: "And what kind of wool do you have, my dear?" I told her I had absolutely none. "Then," she said, laughingly, "I suggest you get some. If you can in this God-forsaken place—" And, with an airy wave of her gloved hand in the direction of the top of my head, she walked away.

So that, I thought, was that. All that courage, all that loss of pride for nothing.

That same blasted wind blew the smell of roasting sunflower seeds my way and, feeling the need to torture myself further, I ambled toward it.

"Little girl, little girl—"

I turned and saw Marya Nikolayevna holding something reddish in her hand.

"Can you make a sweater out of this, little girl?"

Almost in a trance, I went closer and saw that the object she was holding up was a filthy, old, badly torn machine-knitted skirt. If it had been chain mail, I would have said yes.

"Are you sure?" Marya Nikolayevna sounded somewhat sharp.

"Absolutely." In this case, desperation was the mother of conviction.

"And we can settle the price now?"

"Oh, yes."

"You do not have to consult your mother?"

"Certainly not." I lifted my quivering chin.

"So! Let me see—" By now educated in the ways of the *baracholka*, I detected the gleam of the sly and compulsive bargainer and I waited apprehensively. "Let me see—I will pay with a bag of flour, a pail of good potatoes, and, since I just today bought a cow, I will also pay with several liters of milk." She smiled as if her generosity were an adorable weakness.

It had been shrewd of this lady to fix this niggardly price with a child. Mother would have taken the measure of the coat, the earrings, and the new cow and driven a hard bargain with the rich lady of the village. As for me, though I reasoned that with such riches this lady was truly a millionaire, my pride kept me from bargaining.

Not that Mother wasn't still proud too, but it was a pride that was being battered, eroded—and changed—by the years in Siberia. Her pride would not permit her to ask for help from Uncle Yozia, but it did not stop her from bargaining with the best of them on the *baracholka*.

In the shelter of a stall where meat was being sold, Marya Nikolayevna opened her coat and I took her measurements. I used a piece of string that I got by combing two of her bundles; with painstaking care, I measured her arm, her bosom, her waist, her back, and the length, making knots in the string for each measurement. To play safe, and to retain the order in my mind, I measured her twice. I felt very professional.

I took the filthy rag of a skirt from her and thanked God for the gift. Clutching my treasure to me, I raced home indifferent to the wind and the approaching storm: I was racing toward a liter of bitter Siberian milk.

Much to my annoyance, Mother wrinkled her nose fastidiously at the sight of the filthy rag, and had harsh words for high and mighty ladies who expected a child to make a silk purse out of a sow's ear plucked from a garbage can. Even Grandmother looked dubious and wondered if Marya Nikolayevna weren't playing a practical joke on me.

I held back my tears and went to work. Nervously using the precious cake of soap from Uncle Yozia, I washed the filthy, torn skirt. To my delight, little by little a clear, beautiful red emerged from the mud. I waved the skirt triumphantly under the noses of my detractors.

But my triumph was short-lived. What surely became the most tedious and nerve-wracking task of my life began. Inch by inch—or rather stitch by stitch—I ripped the skirt and tied together hundreds of tiny bits of yarn. Nothing in God's name but my empty stomach could have induced me to carry on this nightmare. Mostly I worked at night as I had done when I knitted the sweater for the little girl. As I sat in the semidarkness ripping the wool, I clung to a vision of lovely white flour, potatoes in the peak of their perfection, and milk as rich and golden as any that ever flowed from a prize cow. Sometimes when I thought I could not rip one more row or tie one more knot, I extended the vision to include a bonus from my extremely grateful patron—a quite small piece of juicy beef or perhaps two eggs.

At last it was over, the ripping and the tying. As I gazed at the balls of bright red yarn, scratchy with knots, that I had created so laboriously, I could scarcely bear to unwind one to cast the first stitch.

Once again I was knitting, knitting without a minute to spare for reading, for pleasure, or for playing—throwing snowballs with Svetlana and the other children or chasing each other in the moonlight. This time I even knitted while I studied, with a schoolbook propped up against the small kerosene lamp, and when the kerosene ran out, I knitted in the dark. Sometimes I didn't mind the knitting. Sometimes I even enjoyed it, particularly the sight of rows of knit and rows of purl growing into a pattern, taking on the shape of a sweater. Often I kept myself from falling asleep by celebrating the end of a row of knitting with a chant: "One more potato, one more sip of milk. One more cup of flour, one more sip of milk."

When I was finished with the knitting I had to make the sweater look as if it had been made from brand-new wool. This meant that each and every one of those hundreds of knots had to be made to disappear by pushing them back and weaving their ends into the body of the sweater. I was terrified that one knot might cost me the milk, flour, and potatoes.

To the best of my knowledge—and Grandmother's and Mother's—not one single knot had been left to displease Marya Nikolayevna. The nightmare was over; after weeks of work, the sweater was finished and even Mother, who was sparing with compliments, had to admit that I had made something nice out of garbage. Grandmother, more indulgent, said it was nothing less than a miracle. And I was rather immodestly inclined to agree with her.

Grandmother made a special trip to the *baracholka* to tell Marya Nikolayevna that her sweater was ready. And when would it be convenient for her to receive it? Grandmother asked—in her grandest manner, she assured us in telling us the story later, not for one minute letting on that our stomachs were aching for the payment due. But Marya Nikolayevna did not want me to come to her house, she would come to ours. Mother thought it was because I would see how rich she was and how meanly she had paid me; Grandmother thought the opposite— that she was ashamed of her house, that I would discover that all her wealth was on her back, that she was putting on airs. I chose to be more generous: Marya Nikolayevna was a very thoughtful lady, who did not wish the maker of a marvelous miracle to freeze to death making a delivery.

I waited for Marya Nikolayevna in a state of perpetual motion. I ran back and forth from the window to the bed. I had spread a white sheet on the bed to show off the redness and the beautiful design of the sweater.

Alone in the hut, I prayed aloud for Marya Nikolayevna to like this sweater.

At last, she arrived. I opened the door, and although I had almost lost the habit, I curtsied. The curtsy produced a regal nod as Marya Nikolayevna swept into the hut with all the grandeur of a Leningrad lady used to finer establishments. She tossed her seal coat onto the only chair in the room. In this hut, her earrings sparkled brighter than ever; her *sapogy*—exactly the boots I craved—were brand-new and white as the snow outside. I looked down at our mud floor with its centerpiece of logs, fearful that one stray unpacked speck of dirt would fly onto those gorgeous boots. Marya Nikolayevna was looking too—at the mud floor, the logs, the beds, and the makeshift stove; she was looking as if she had never seen the inside of a Siberian hut before and as if she very much did not like what she saw, as if it filled her with revulsion, pity, and scorn.

Anna Karenina? Yes, here were the full, round shoulders, the dark hair with the ringlets framing her face, the fair, luminous skin. But missing in Marya Nikolayevna's face were Anna's kind gray eyes, the softness which I now longed for. Instead, the slightly slanted eyes that were inspecting the hut were black polished to a steely brilliance—hard eyes.

I began to storm inside. I hated pity and too early in life I had learned that pity and scorn had an attraction for each other. After all, this hut was spotlessly clean and the gauze curtains were a pretty yellow. Why hadn't she noticed *that*?

But my growing anger was short-lived. I had something much more devastating to contend with than pity and scorn. Something much more important to observe than Marya Nikolayevna's resemblance to or difference from Anna Karenina.

What I saw before me was beyond belief, created only in a nightmare.

"Well, my child, so my sweater is finished at long last."

The voice was the voice heard in the echo chamber of nightmare.

Fat!

Marya Nikolayevna had gotten *fat!* Pounds and pounds heavier.

"Yes, ma'am." I spoke in a choked whisper.

It couldn't be; not after the weeks of work. I must be seeing things.

I picked up the sweater without looking at it, the

child in me, no doubt, counting on magic for the sweater to grow fat and big like Marya Nikolayevna.

"Shall I help you with it?" I asked, still unable to speak above a whisper.

"Yes, of course."

Marya Nikolayevna raised one arm and put it into a sleeve. Tight, very tight, but in. Then the other white and pretty hand was drawn through the second sleeve. I smoothed out the back, pulling it a little this way and more than a little the other way. Somehow I managed to walk around to the front.

"*Esinka!*" The voice was now all too present, dangerously emerged from the unreality of nightmare. "*Esinka!* This sweater does not fit at all. It will not close. It is much, much too tight!"

My feet buckled under me. I saw spots as brilliantly red as the sweater.

"Marya Nikolayevna, it can't be small! It can't be! I measured you and I measured the sweater . . . it has to be right, it just has to be. . . ."

I was fighting my hysteria with all my strength; Marya Nikolayevna must not see me cry; she must never know how much the milk and flour and potatoes meant to us. I swallowed hard and took a few deep breaths.

"My dear child," Marya Nikolayevna went on in her slow, smooth way, "haven't you forgotten something?"

What was she talking about? What could I possibly have forgotten? The sweater had everything a sweater ought to have—a back, a front, everything.

"Forgotten?"

"Forgotten. Think!"

Marya Nikolayevna was smiling. She was playing a game, one she was enjoying immensely. My throat tightened unbearably. In another second I would cry. I shook my head.

"The cow, my dove, the cow."

"The cow," I repeated foolishly.

"My dear child, the cow I bought that day turned out to be a very good cow. Her milk has made me nice and fat. If only you had remembered! But do not look so sad, I am not angry with you. You will simply redo the sweater."

I could not speak. I took the sweater off, peeling it from Marya Nikolayevna's plump shoulders and fat arms as if I were ripping bandages off my own raw skin. I laid it back on the white sheet, straightening it out and smoothing it as I did so.

"Now, if you will excuse me, my dove, I must go," she said. "And when shall I come back for the sweater?"

Feeling as if I were sentencing myself to life imprisonment, I muttered, ". . . perhaps . . . I think . . . perhaps in two months . . ."

When the door closed after her, I sat down on the bed beside the sweater. I picked it up and put it on my lap. I allowed myself to weep. I wept for the wasted weeks and I wept for the potatoes and the flour and the milk we were not to get. When I thought of the milk, I thought of the good cow. Suddenly I hated that good cow as I had never hated anything in my life. And while I was at it, I decided to be angry at the earth that would not feed us. And at myself for crying like a baby.

"Stop crying," I said aloud. "And start ripping."

But I couldn't. It was too soon to destroy my miracle.

By the time Mother came home, I had stopped crying but when I saw her I began all over again. She listened to me tell my story between sobs and sniffles.

"Oh, you poor thing . . ."she began and then before my astonished eyes, I saw that she was restraining her own hysteria—hysterical laughter, that is.

I was outraged.

"But, darling . . ." the tears were rolling down her cheeks ". . . the irony of it. You were so happy about that cow. And look what it did to you. . . ."

CHAPTER 16

That winter, cold settled in the bones as if it would be stored there indefinitely like ice in an icehouse.

The hut was perpetually cold. I ripped the red sweater with ice-cold fingers and a cold heart, and when it was too cold to stay out of bed, I knitted in bed, wearing socks (old socks of Father's had replaced my outgrown ones), my sweater, and often a shawl over my head. I tried wearing gloves but that didn't work.

In the early morning when it was still dark, the moment of leaving the cold hut for the walk to school was always a moment of trauma. The walk would take well over an hour and it wasn't a walk at all; it was a constant battle with a ferociously buffeting and icy wind. The battle might have been lost if I had not gone in convoy. The convoy consisted of about six children who picked one another up on the way and used one another as windbreaks. Holding on to our books with one arm, we grabbed one another around the waist with the free arm and hid behind one another's backs. For once, no one wanted to be the leader and we took turns being first in line. On the way we would meet other little bands of children linked together. Everyone who could went to school this way in the Siberian winter; no one was ever excluded; everyone was needed. In this instance, if there was a most popular person, it would be the biggest and the fattest.

There was one place where I forgot the cold, indeed forgot Siberia. That was in the library. There, in that muddy village, was a great institution. Not physically to be sure, but in every other way imaginable. It was a small log cabin, immaculately attended to with loving care; it was well lighted with oil lamps and it was *warm*. But best of all, it contained a small but amazing collection from the world's best literature, truly amazing considering the time, the place, and its size. From floor to ceiling it was lined with books—books, books, books. It was there that I was to become acquainted with the works of Dumas, Pasternak's translations of Shakespeare, the novels of Mark Twain, Jack London, and of course the Russians. It was in that log cabin that I escaped from Siberia—either reading there or taking the books home. It was between that library and two extraordinary teachers that I developed a lifelong passion for the great Russian novelists and poets. It was there that I learned to line up patiently for my turn to sit at a table and read, to wait—sometimes months—for a book. It was there that I learned that reading was not only a great delight, but a *privilege*.

Cold or no cold, fearing that I might still be running a race with the cow, I finally finished the red sweater. And promptly got myself another customer. This time it was a lady who had come from Moscow with her daughter—and some wool. Lovely, fluffy, soft, unused wool. The lady ordered two sweaters and agreed to pay me with a chifforobe.

"A what?" Mother wanted to know.

"A chifforobe, Mama. It's just *beautiful*."

"And just what we need, I suppose?"

I seemed to need it. I loved it. It was made of plywood and it had been stained brown; it had a cupboard on top and two drawers below. We had some difficulty fitting it into the hut: its front rested on the logs covering the hole so that it stood somewhat tilted. And there wasn't too much that we owned to put in it; in fact, it was rather pathetically empty. But I thought it was beautiful and that I had been well paid.

One night the hut got too cold for Mother. In the country of permafrost, subzero temperatures, and snow as deep as a hut is high, a glass of water turned to ice should have been of no consequence, but it was. Every night Mother set a glass of water down beside her bed; the night that she awakened with a thirst to find that the water had turned to ice was the last straw. She was certain we would all freeze to death in that hut and she decided to enlist Uncle Yozia's help in finding a new home.

Uncle Yozia and Aunt Zaya had become more and more important, not just to me but to Mother too. Indeed, there were ways in which she needed them even more than I did. I had school and homework and school friends to remind me that I was still a member of the human race, but not so Mother. If it had not been for a few Polish families and most particularly Uncle Yozia and Aunt Zaya, I think it more than likely that Mother would have cracked up. Good talk was her beauty treatment; the life would come back to her, bringing with it her old beauty. She and Uncle Yozia and Aunt Zaya talked about everything in the warmth and coziness of their living room. Cozy, that is, by Siberian standards, where a decent fire, one rug, and possibly one or two overstuffed chairs gave one the illusion of opulence. They talked about Turgenev, a great favorite of Mother's, and Sholem Aleichem. They talked about music. They compared notes about the things they had seen and done. But they did not talk about politics or about any aspect of Soviet life that derived from its social system. They talked as if they were in a café in Vilna or Paris or London, as if the next day were not certain to bring some confrontation with sickness or starvation or death, or all three. And usually there was some rationed tea and some precious tidbit, such as a piece of smoked red fish, to add to the pleasure.

Thanks to Uncle Yozia's concern, we were offered the possibility of a few months' respite from cold and hunger; in other words, a sojourn in heaven. One of the directors of the tractor factory, Yosif Isayevich, would give us food (in addition to our own rations) and lodging in exchange for caring for him and his house while his wife and children were away. His house was warm and clean and there would even be eggs to eat. But—

The "but" was a staggering one and stuck in Uncle Yozia's throat: there would be no room for Grandmother. Mother and I were adamant: it was out of the question for us to be separated.

Grandmother was equally adamant: it was stupid for three people to freeze to death, particularly when two of them could invite the third one to warm her bones at their fire and share food. "Besides, we can use a little holiday from each other." That was true; they were human and the long, close confinement under dreadful conditions had been a strain on both Grandmother and Mother. It could not have been otherwise, but to me in Siberia togetherness was everything, and I felt not only guilty, but betrayed.

The Kaftals had found a hut for themselves, quite as miserable as ours, and Grandmother was to sleep there. Taking Grandmother and her little bundles to the Kaftals' made me feel sick.

"We shouldn't have let her," I said to Mother.

"Stop it!" Mother said sharply. "I don't need you to make me feel any worse than I do."

Yosif Isayevich's house was next to the tractor factory. When we moved, my precious chifforobe came along too; and very useful it was, since it served to divide our sleeping quarters from Yosif Isayevich's in his two-room (bedroom and kitchen) house.

Yosif Isayevich was a genial man who shared his food generously, kept his wooden house warm, and treated Mother with great respect. So much so, that when he was drunk, which was often, his chief concern was to keep it a secret from Mother. "Please—" he said to me once when he came home drunk in the afternoon, "I beg of you, do not let your mother know. Such a fine lady . . ." Not letting Mother know must have given him a much-bruised shin; it meant that he would come home late, when he thought we would be asleep. And we would lie there, listening to him bump about in the dark, and hope that he wouldn't break a leg. It was a ludicrous game.

Whatever we did for him, we did because we wanted to, not because he demanded it. We cooked and we cleaned and I learned how to iron a man's shirt. I ironed on a blanket-covered board, which was placed across the backs of two chairs, and I used an iron filled with hot coals, blowing on them to keep them burning.

Yosif Isayevich's house was wired for electricity, but as we stared up into an empty socket we were constantly reminded of the scarcity of bulbs. However, there was a loud-speaker in the kitchen and the government-sponsored broadcasts brought us news from the outside world and music—opera, folk songs, and dance music. Sitting in Yosif Isayevich's warm kitchen, listening to music, Mother and I would be filled with wonder at our good fortune. Grandmother did come to eat with us and that winter all three of us got a little fatter.

CHAPTER 17

When the announcement was made in school that there was to be a declamation contest the following August, the devil—or the ham in me—prodded me into entering it.

Raisa Nikitovna gave out a list of works from which the students were to make their selections. As usual, there were the poems about the glories of the Soviet Union and the Stakhanov workers. Odes to Stalin, to the Russian soldiers, and a sonnet or two to the Soviet people. And way down at the bottom of the list, as if it were a frivolous afterthought not to be taken too seriously, was Pushkin's *Eugene Onegin*.

I loved *Onegin*. I loved it for taking me from my harsh exile back to a time and a place I never knew, to its lost world.

In the past two years, Raisa Nikitovna had not become any friendlier; on the contrary, she seemed to have interred herself in a cake of ice. She among all my teachers still made me feel like an outsider and with her my Polish accent was always at its heaviest. I hated having to ask her for permission to enter the contest.

"You wish to recite an ode to our great leader, Stalin?" she asked, her face smooth as ice and her voice sharp with sarcasm.

She had a point, of course.

I confessed that—with her kind permission—I would like to attempt Tatyana's dream from *Eugene Onegin*.

A frown cracked the ice. Clearly, Raisa Nikitovna thought it inappropriate for a Polish deportee to have the honor of entering a Soviet declamation contest, no matter what she declaimed.

"Are you aware that there are to be no prizes?" she asked, reducing me to some greedy little monster. (Grandmother was more explicit: "Anti-Semite!" she cried.)

If I had had any sense I would have given up then, but I came from a long line of stubborn idiots.

So I began to study Tatyana's dream as if I were preparing for a performance at the Bolshoi Theater. Tatyana is a shy country girl who falls in love with a worldly man from St. Petersburg society, Eugene Onegin. Her terrifying dream foreshadows the tragic future of her love.

It was my objective that Tatyana and I become one, nothing less. So I memorized, recited, read, performed in front of anyone who cared—or did not care—to listen. I tried out every nuance of speech, worked on every word. No one escaped my histrionics—my friends, Mother's friends, not even a hawk soaring over the deserted steppe.

" 'An awesome dream Tatyana's dreaming . . .' "

The hundredth, the two-hundredth time?

Even my poor grandmother began to wilt when she came to visit us.

"Beautiful, beautiful . . ." she said. "But so frightening . . . the bear . . . and the wood . . . and those freaks . . . Esther, darling, such a marvelous actress you are, you're frightening your poor old grandmother. Better stop, darling—"

Would Sarah Bernhardt have stopped? I went on and on through that spring at Yosif Isayevich's being Tatyana with her dream and her great sad love for Eugene Onegin.

Late in the spring I was temporarily interrupted.

Life at Yosif Isayevich's had been pleasant, comparatively speaking. Letters from Father were reassuring and when it was planting time, when we were to be assigned a piece of barren soil to struggle with, Yosif Isayevich told us that we need not worry about potatoes, that more than likely we would be spending another winter with him. And if not, he would help us out.

But Yosif Isayevich's wife returned much sooner than expected and the hunt was on again. After the usual difficulties, we ended up back in the village with a young couple and a baby. Their mud hut had one room and a kitchen, which kindhearted Yosif Isayevich arranged to have divided in half, giving Mother and me a tiny place to sleep. So tiny that there was only room enough for a narrow bed for one person, Mother. Squeezed between my chifforobe and the wall was a small blanket chest for me to sleep on. It was too short for me to stretch out full length; when I did so, I put my feet up on the wall in the beauty position. But since the chest backed the stove on the other side of the wall, it would be a lovely foot warmer in the winter.

Once we were settled in our new hut, it was the young couple, Natasha and Nikolay, and the little baby, Katia, who became my best audience:

"'An awesome dream Tatyana's dreaming . . .'" I recited.

The baby thought I was absolutely splendid.

Nervous and excited in equal parts, I spent the whole night before the declamation contest awake in my cramped bed. Feet higher than my head, belly caved in, I swung from the exalted moment when my ears would ring with the shouts of bravo, shouts that would eventually lead me to the stages of Moscow, Leningrad, Warsaw, and New York, down to the ghastly moment when I would stand up in the school auditorium the victim of total amnesia.

That August was hot. Sometimes so hot that our cozy little corner in Natasha and Nikolay's hut made me feel as if we were buried alive in a bed of steaming manure.

As soon as morning came, I crept out for a breath of fresh air before the others awakened. The dew was lifting from the parched steppe, shrouding the huts of the village.

I knew it was going to be another scorcher, but who cared about the heat? Who cared about anything but the contest?

And what was I going to wear?

Almost from the beginning, from the time I had signed up for the contest, this question had recurred as it must to every female who ever lived. And like every female who ever lived, I expected some fairy, the one assigned to these matters, to do her duty.

I tiptoed into the hut and pulled my clothes out of the chifforobe and took them back outside.

I set them on the ground and looked at them. The fairy had been otherwise occupied. All that lay there before me to choose between was my cotton dress, the one and only one I had left, now faded and threadbare, and a woolen skirt patched in many places, with the ubiquitous heavy red and blue sweater.

I held the dress up against myself, as if I didn't know. I pressed the dress close to my body and looked down. As if I didn't know from wearing it day in and day out that it was much much too short. I made my decision; all at once I knew what it would feel like to stand up in the auditorium in a dress that exposed my bony knees —half naked is what it would feel like.

Oh, why hadn't I been my own good fairy and grabbed a party dress or two that morning in Vilna? the pale blue organdy? I saw the closet in my room in Vilna with my party dresses hanging together, each one a souvenir of parties and plays and concerts, each one a souvenir of laughter and wonder. I saw the white wool dress and my lacquered shoes, and recalled that I had worn them to my first opera. Suddenly I heard the opening of the overture and I remembered that the first opera had been *Eugene Onegin!* Was this a good or a bad omen?

"What are you doing out here? Why are you up so early?" Mother came out of the hut, combing her hair.

How could Mama have forgotten? I wanted to know. (Well, how *could* she have? Had she thought that she had been forever doomed to listen to Tatyana's dream?)

"Once more, Mama. Please listen to the poem just once more."

"My dear child, word for word Pushkin himself never knew this poem as well as you do. Now I must get dressed and go to work. . . ."

I must have looked so stricken that Mother said, "Just once more, Esther—while I wash and dress."

I trailed after her to our room.

The room was too small and Mother sloshing water over her face was a poor audience. I stumbled over a word and it filled me with panic. What came next?

"Oh, God! This is terrible, terrible, *terrible!*" I cried.

"The more terrible it is now, the better you will be later," Mother said calmly.

This was a most unlikely thing for Mother, the pessimist and the perfectionist, to say. Overwrought though I was, it fascinated me. How could she say such a thing?

"In the theater it is a well-known fact," Mother said, "that the worse a dress rehearsal goes, the better the opening performance."

True, Mother had known some famous actors and actresses in Vilna. I was willing to be convinced of that well-known fact, but by no means did it take care of Raisa Nikitovna.

"And what about her, for goodness' sake?" Mother asked.

"If she is one of the judges, I'm finished. She hates me."

Mother stopped fixing her hair. Mother was not an effusive mother, nor a demonstrative one, but the idea of *anyone*, the devil himself, hating *her* child was too ridiculous for words.

"Stop being so silly," she snapped.

Silly or not, I thought, she doesn't really know Raisa Nikitovna. None of us children had been able to find out who the judges were to be and this anonymous body had become our common bugaboo. But I felt that Raisa Nikitovna was my personal enemy. I wasn't going to argue with Mother, but I hoped and prayed that Raisa Nikitovna was miles and miles away from that contest, preferably on the other side of the Urals.

One by one they left the hut, wishing me good luck —Mother, then Nikolay and Natasha, taking Katia with them to the day nursery at the factory where they worked. To them this would be just another day, hot and parched and difficult. Nothing special, nothing earth-shaking, nothing beautiful was likely to happen to them that day. But to me, it might; my whole life might be changed that day.

I sat down on my bed. The tension and the excitement had made me dizzy, or perhaps the hunger. When the world stopped whirling, I looked at my nails. This morning I was supposed to spread a fresh layer of yellow clay on the ground in our room to make it clean. For once I wanted no telltale signs under my nails and on my knees to advertise that we had no floor, for once I would be a bad housekeeper.

I washed my hands and feet, put on the skirt and sweater, and dug out the chipped mirror Anya had passed on to me. A white face with apprehensive eyes peered back at me. Not having seen myself in a mirror for a long time, I saw the face of a stranger. A fine Tatyana I'd make! To put a smile on that mournful face in the mirror, I stuck my tongue out and made devil's horns behind my head. It worked; I smiled— wanly. I had let my hair grow again and I pulled at it, trying to get the knots out. I yanked some hairs from my head and used them to tie my braids.

It was time to go.

The road to school was longer and hotter than usual. The huts were already baking in the sun, seeming to dry up before one's eyes. My sweater was drenched with perspiration and the dust that covered my freshly washed feet had spread up over my legs, had even flown up to my skirt. I went past the *baracholka* where already someone was haggling over what looked like a torn sheet. Down at the creek, I could see that a little boy waited patiently for a fish to present itself in the trickle that was all the drought had left of the waters.

When I saw the blaze of white that was the school, I felt a rush of happiness that momentarily dissolved my fears. This was the morning I had been preparing for for months. In an hour Tatyana and I would be one.

I was early, the first to arrive for the contest. I couldn't decide whether to go in alone or wait for one of my friends. I went in alone. But not before brushing the dust off my skirt and pulling the sweater away from my overheated body as much as possible.

The front door opened with a creak. The corridor was quiet and the floor was freshly scrubbed. In here it was cooler and I took a deep breath. I crept along the hall, as if the floor were made of glass, until I reached the largest classroom in the school, the one we used as an auditorium.

The door was partly open and I could see the improvised platform and the rows of chairs. The room appeared to be empty and I went in.

It was not empty. Standing at a table, arranging some papers, was Raisa Nikitovna. Her mousy hair had been drawn back tighter than I had ever seen it. Not by so much as a raised eyebrow did she give any sign of seeing me.

"Pardon me, Raisa Nikitovna . . ."

Two slivers of granite, gray and cold, were turned my way.

"Yes, what is it?"

Cold, cold.

"Why . . . why, I'm here for the contest . . ."

She shuffled the papers on the table. "I don't recall seeing your name on any of these lists."

I thought I would die right then and there. I didn't die, but I did begin to tremble.

"But, Raisa Nikitovna, don't you remember . . . ? I'm the one who's doing Tatyana's dream? Please . . . don't you remember . . . ?"

At last she found my name, obviously regretting that she had done so.

"Let me look at you," she said.

I stood straight as a needle, with my shoulders back, my head raised high, and my eyes just above Raisa Nikitovna's head, avoiding her face.

"You cannot appear on the stage this morning, this way. Not under any circumstances."

Dear God, why not? Now what have I done?

"Look at yourself. Whatever made you think you could go up on that stage in front of your teachers, judges, visitors that way?"

"What way, please?"

"What way, please? Without your shoes, of course. That's what way."

So that was it. No shoes. I looked down and saw a pair of dirty feet. Where had they come from, these dirty, shoeless feet? Who owned them anyway?

I found my voice. "I am so sorry, Raisa Nikitovna. I completely forgot to put my shoes on. I guess the excitement of the contest . . . I'll run . . . run . . . right back to our house and put my shoes on. I'll be back before the contest is all over. Will that be all right with you?"

"See that you come back on time. We shall not wait for you."

And with those words she turned away to straighten a chair that was not in need of being straightened.

I ran out of the school.

My panic was total. I had no shoes. The school shoes with which I had dragged my feet out of our house in Vilna that morning had long since become too small even for a child's feet in Siberia and had been sold for a hunk of bread. What was I to do? I thought of borrowing a pair from a friend, but who among them owned more than one pair? No one. If only we had not been so proud and had let Uncle Yozia . . . someplace, somehow he would have found a pair. . . .

My only hope was that I would find something in our hut—something belonging to Mother or to Natasha, or even to Nikolay.

I ran. As I ran, I held back tears of bewilderment along with the panic. Why did one need shoes to speak? And why did Raisa Nikitovna hate me so much?

When I reached the hut, I didn't stop to catch my breath but immediately pulled out Mother's clothes. To my great relief, I found a pair of old felt slippers she must have picked up at the *baracholka*. Clutching them to my chest, I thanked God for them. I would not be barefoot. I slipped my feet into them. They were enormous, so enormous that they fell off my feet with the first step. Frantically I searched for a piece of string and when I found it I ran from the hut, leaving everything topsy-turvy.

With the slippers under my arm and the string clutched tightly in one fist, I raced back over the dusty road. My throat was dry as paper and the dust stung my eyes. But on I ran as if I were possessed. I almost collided with an old man who was walking peacefully along the road. He stared at me—a wild creature clutching slippers and swinging a clenched fist madly in the air. He shook his head from side to side when I called out, "Excuse me, *diedushka*." The poor Polish kid has gone berserk, he seemed to think.

I could scarcely breathe by the time I got back to school. Each breath escaped with a huge rasping noise.

My shoulders heaved and my knees trembled. My braids had loosened and hair was falling over my eyes. But I had returned. With the inside edge of my skirt I wiped the dust from my toes and ankles and slipped my feet into the slippers. I tied them with the string and opened the door into the corridor.

The string just about kept the slippers on my feet, but as I ran toward the auditorium like a deranged duck, the corridor echoed with the clop, clop, clopping of the slippers.

Trying to keep the door from squeaking, I slid into the auditorium. The door did squeak and all eyes turned toward me. Except those of a boy who was on the stage reciting an ode to Stalin in a high, nasal voice.

Raisa Nikitovna sat next to the table looking at me with eyes more like granite than ever.

"Oh, so you're back," she whispered, somehow making a whisper sound like a snarl. "Walk over . . ." She started to point to the other side of the table, then she saw the slippers. "Is that what you call—?" My heart stopped beating for one second. Raisa Nikitovna looked up from the slippers. She looked at my face. "You will follow Grisha. You are the last contestant." She pointed to a single empty chair and I waddled toward it.

I had barely sat down when the boy Grisha finished the ode and Raisa Nikitovna called my name.

Still struggling with my breath, I walked over to the stage and climbed the three steps leading to the platform. I nearly lost one slipper. Someone snickered.

I reached the center of the platform. I took one last deep breath:

" 'An awesome dream Tatyana's dreaming . . .' "

I could not lift my eyes from the floor; I was too tired.

The words came, one after another, in their proper sequence. That was all. Pushkin's poetry was gone. Nothing was left of its color, its spirit.

I kept on going. Near the end, I lifted my eyes from the floor. The audience was a big, gray blur. I was so tired. But in a way, a way I had not anticipated, Tatyana and I had become one; we were together in a nightmare.

Floating toward me from the gray blur was the face of Raisa Nikitovna. A face I had never seen before. The cold, forbidding stare was gone and in its place there seemed to be a grudging respect. And strangest of all, some kindness too.

At last I finished. What little applause there was was weak and short-lived.

I walked off the stage and sat down, grateful for something to sit on. I closed my eyes and waited for the judges to make their decision.

A girl named Katiusha won.

The contest was over.

Avoiding my friends, I walked slowly back to the hut, kicking the dust with my bare toes.

I would put Mother's slippers back and I would never tell her about the high cost of going barefoot.

But I was determined to get myself a pair of shoes—somehow, someplace.

CHAPTER 18

There was a man in the village who was always receiving "Red Cross packages from abroad"—clothing and food in great profusion which he was suspected of bartering or selling at exorbitant prices. We all suspected him of being an informer for the police.

Shortly after the declamation contest, I heard that this man had received some Bally shoes from Switzerland. Shoes had become such an obsession with me that automatically, without pausing to think, I made a beeline for his house.

Under the spell of my obsession, not bothering to be

polite, l came directly to the point: I needed a pair of shoes. And I needed them badly. I talked fast and furiously and held up one dirty foot to prove my point. He looked startled. He hemmed and hawed and studied my bare feet and then told me to come the next day and he would see what he could do.

For weeks on end, I went to his house every day. I had drawn the outline of my feet to show my shoe size on a piece of old newspaper and left it with him. "Maybe tomorrow I'll find a pair . . ."

Finally, to stop my daily nagging, he produced a pair of navy-blue shoes with prewar rubber soles. I thought they were the most beautiful things I had ever seen. Never mind that they pinched just a little bit.

The shoes worked; merely possessing them made me feel rich, elegant, and the equal of anyone in the village. As for wearing them, this I did only rarely, on very special occasions. When one owned such beautiful shoes, one could afford to go barefoot. But when I did wear them, as I walked the dusty roads I stopped every other step to wipe them with the edge of my dress. I used to come home from these walks with a dusty hem, but shining shoes.

It would be more accurate to say that the shoes made me feel *almost* the equal of anyone.

That summer Uncle Yozia had had me registered at the new school that was being built in the *novostroyka* for the children of the factory's directors and workers. It would be a much better school, he said, and since he had pulled more than one string to get me in, I was reluctant to tell him that an old familiar school was better than the best new school. Besides, now that we were back in the village, I would have more than an hour's walk each way.

He and Aunt Zaya introduced me to the children of the "big wheels" of the factory before school started and the experience was painful. These children who had come from European Russia had not known the hardship of life in Siberia and, being the children of the elite, were in fact spared much of it. Like children everywhere, they stuck together, played together, had their own slang. They were not impressed with my new shoes. With them, once again I felt as I did when we first came to Siberia, once again I was the outsider.

The new school was a long, wooden, barrackslike building, much larger than the village school. As far as I was concerned, the most impressive thing about this building was that it was *warm*. School started in September and by October we had had our first snowstorm. After more than an hour's walk through the dark village, over the windy steppe, in clothes that had never been meant for an arctic climate, the first moments inside school were always filled with the purely sensual pleasure of thawing out. In this school, we did not have to sit all day in our coats and mittens and when it was time to go home in the afternoon, it took courage to plunge into the huge, ice-cold Siberian twilight.

It was in this school that I was to meet some truly great teachers. Almost all of them had taught in the universities in European Russia and had been forced to flee the German armies. They were generous with their knowledge and their classes were more than an adventure in learning; these men and women transported us from a remote Siberian village to the heart of Leningrad and Moscow, whetting our appetites for theater and ballet and music—and books, of course.

I was happy to find two familiar faces among the children. Katiusha—who had won the contest—was here, and although she was the daughter of a director and lived in one of the splendid apartments and was well aware of her status, we became moderately good friends. It was considered an honor to be counted her friend. The other girl was Zina. Zina felt herself to be the honored one if she had any friends, even one as socially inconsequential as I. She was the daughter of a Russian Jewish widow who had fled from the invading Germans and seemed still to be looking over her shoulder, still fleeing. I remember Zina as being the palest child I had ever seen. But amazingly enough, floating above her paleness was a brilliant mane of chestnut hair, gleaming with lights one rarely saw in Siberia. Zina and I never talked about how much we wanted to be accepted by the others; we pretended that we didn't care. But our nonacceptance was our closest bond.

The fall winds brought Mother and me the ugly smell of starvation. Once again we were about to face winter with an empty larder. Foolishly, we had accepted Yosif Isayevich's assurance that we need not worry about food. He still offered to help, but since his wife proved to be anything but generous, Mother—to my dismay and confusion—politely refused.

To make matters worse, Mother was transferred from the bakery where she had gotten some bread rations to a construction job in the *novostroyka*. There the work was hard, the pay small, and she too had the long difficult walk each day.

I had almost had my fill of knitting. But we had met a dressmaker through Uncle Yozia and Aunt Zaya, a perky little lady named Alexandra Lvovna, who made clothes for the wives of the factory directors.

Since she lived near school, I stopped in one afternoon to offer my services. I could crochet collars and cuffs and dickies for her customers' dresses, I told her.

"And how do you expect to be paid?" she asked, sizing me up and down.

When I told her that she need only pay me after I had proved my worth with work satisfactorily done, she agreed to try me when the opportunity arose. It was decided that Katiusha, who lived near Alexandra Lvovna, would be the messenger.

Pleased that everything had been settled so easily, I put out my hand. "Good-by, Madame Lvovna," I said.

"*Madame* Lvovna?" she asked, narrowing her eyes.

"Oh, please forgive me," I said quickly. "It's just that my mother used to call our dressmaker at home 'madame' and I thought it was the thing to do—"

"Madame Lvovna?" she repeated, now cocking her head to one side.

"You don't like that?"

"As a matter of fact, I do." She began to laugh. "Sounds more like a dressmaker than Comrade Lvovna, doesn't it?"

Oh, no, I thought, I'm not such an innocent as to be trapped into criticizing the Soviet way.

I kept my mouth shut and shrugged.

One Monday, Katiusha told me that Alexandra Lvovna had work for me. I went directly to her house after school and picked up some blue fabric and pink thread. I was to make a collar and cuff set and a little handkerchief by crocheting pink lace edges around the blue fabric. I was thrilled with this order and promised to bring it back on Sunday without fail.

By Sunday they were ready.

I told Mother that I was going to Alexandra Lvovna's to deliver the things.

In Siberia in the winter, before one traveled any distance at all, one studied the skies. Mother went to the window that Sunday afternoon.

"No," she said. "You are not to go. The sky is too dark on the horizon. I think there will be a storm."

I looked too but all I could see were the rubles Alexandra Lvovna was going to give me and the piece of meat I would buy that very day—and who knew? perhaps a glass of sunflower seeds too. I protested that I absolutely had to go, that there was not going to be any storm, and that if there was I could outrun it easily. "Please, please, please . . ."

Mother covered her ears against the nagging. "Go, go. You are so stubborn . . ."

Before I left, she made me promise that if it looked dangerous when I reached Alexandra Lvovna's, I would not leave until it was safe, absolutely safe.

When I started down the road toward the *novostroyka*, I could see that behind me, way off in the distant north, there was a smudge of darkness on the horizon. And the air did seem still.

I had an hour's walk ahead of me and I tried to pace myself to walk as fast as possible without getting winded. Walking south, away from that dark smudge, I had more pleasant things to think of than a Siberian storm; walking alone on the steppe was the ideal time for daydreaming.

By the time I reached Alexandra Lvovna's, the dark smudge had in fact disappeared and the sky seemed considerably lighter.

Alexandra Lvovna was pleased with my work and thought she would have more for me soon. I was delighted. This had been much easier than knitting sweaters and one got paid so much faster.

Only one didn't get paid.

"Oh, no, my dear. You will only get paid when I get paid for the dress," Alexandra Lvovna said sweetly.

I felt that she was being dishonest, that she had the money to pay me now.

"But, Alexandra Lvovna . . ." I started to protest and then thought better of it. I wanted more work, needed it desperately, and couldn't afford to argue.

But I left her house in a rage. My fists were clenched and I invoked every curse I had learned—of which there were quite a few—on Alexandra Lvovna's head.

I walked fast, propelled by my rage, oblivious of any storm but the one boiling within me.

I was halfway home when I saw the first signs of danger. As far as the eye could see, all around, wherever I looked, snow was lifting and spiraling from the steppe. This swirling mass of wind-driven snow is called the *buran*. The *buran* in itself, as it rises from the steppe, is dangerous enough; with its whirlpools making one totally blind, it is more dangerous than falling snow. As I stood there for a second, I felt as if the whole huge steppe were revolving under my feet. Then, as it does in Siberia in a great winter storm, the world went black.

The wind blew up with a force that knocked me sideways, and now the snow was coming both from the earth and from the sky. The world was a maniacal, gyrating black funnel of noise and I was in the bottom of it. Alone. Completely alone.

I started to fight my way through this storm. I knew that if I panicked, if I went in circles, if I stopped altogether, I would die. It was as brutally simple as that. Countless people had died this way. One minute's rest could be fatal.

I kept telling myself to push forward, push forward. But with the wind knocking me every which way, I had all I could do to keep on my feet. I was no longer certain that I was going forward. I had lost my sense of direction.

I prayed. Over and over again, I asked God please to help me. I asked Him to spare me. Over and over again I said, I don't want to die, I don't want to die, as if in itself not wanting to die could save my life. Which of course it could.

My prayers had been silent ones. Only once did I call out loud "Oh, God!" Still, I was beginning to lose my breath.

Suddenly, the wind carried a new sound, very faint: the sound of my name. "Esther . . . Esther . . ." it seemed to say. I thought I was going mad. If men went mad on the desert, surely they could in such a storm. . . .

"Esther . . . Esther . . ."

And then something else. I couldn't make out what. Mad or not, I went toward this sound which kept repeating itself. Any step that took me away from it, I counted a wrong step and corrected myself.

"Esther . . . Esther . . ."

And then, "*Sh'mah Israel* . . ."

With every ounce of strength I had left, I forced myself toward that sound.

In the swirling blackness, I saw a figure.

"*Sh'mah Israel* . . ."

Hear, O Israel: The Lord our God, the Lord is One.

I fell into my mother's arms.

There was no doubt about it. She had saved my life.

Standing in the middle of the road, a few yards from our hut, endangering her own life, knowing that I was out there someplace, she had turned herself into a human beam, homing me as surely as if I were a plane being homed in on an electric beam.

Sh'mah Israel . . .

CHAPTER 19

That winter when I was thirteen years old—in the European fashion, thinking of myself as fourteen—the line between Polish deportee and Siberian girl sometimes appeared dangerously close to being extinguished.

Living with Natasha and Nikolay, I almost felt that coming back to the hut from school was coming home.

Natasha was young and gay and seemed to enjoy having me around. She treated me as if I were a younger sister and trusted me with Katia. Still fresh from playing with rag dolls, I adored having a real live one, a plump blond baby girl complete with gurgles and tears. There were no rules and regulations, no theories, no vitamins, no special baby foods, no bottles or pacifiers for Katia. When she cried, she was given a rag soaked in sugar water to suck on. She liked it very much. She didn't seem to mind being swaddled as all Siberian babies were, at least the ones I saw. Natasha taught me how to place Katia in the exact center of a large square woolen shawl and fold it around her till she was wrapped up like a little mummy. Her cradle was next to her parents' bed, suspended from the ceiling. After a while, when our food, Mother's and mine, was in extremely short supply, Natasha would occasionally engage me to take care of the baby in exchange for some food. Then I would sit next to the cradle, rocking it with my knee as I read or did my homework.

And in Natasha's kitchen, I learned how to spin. The spinning wheel was primitive, without a foot pedal; one turned the wheel by hand. The curly dirty gray wool that had come directly from the lambs' backs, instead of being washed first, was smelly and sticky and difficult to work. The idea was to pull the wool gently off the spindle onto the wheel, making the thread as even as possible. Mine never was. But sitting in that kitchen, singing with Natasha who was spinning the wool that she would use for shawls for herself and her baby and her mother, I was happy.

Except when the radio—which Mother and I were thrilled to find here too—brought news from the outside world. The Germans were on their dreadful bloody rampage. Terrified and horrified, I wanted to run from the kitchen, but I sat there listening. Listening, I willed Father to safety.

As for the rest of our family—my other grandmother,

my aunts and uncles, my cousins—I could tell just by looking at Mother's haunted face that another piece of ghastly, incredible news of the continuing genocide had filtered into the village. I looked but I had learned to stop asking questions. Ourselves, we had absolutely no word at all about our family.

Grandmother continued living with the Kaftals and although she visited us almost daily, I missed having her around. Not only did I love her dearly, but her grandmotherly link with the past was more precious than ever.

However, the radio did not just bring war news; blessedly there was still music—the operas, the symphonies, the folk songs, and the dance music.

After considerable dunning on my part, Alexandra Lvovna paid me, a fraction of what she should have; but there was no more work from her. Desperate, I tried to get some more knitting to do, but now there was no wool at all, not even a dirty old skirt to be ripped, and Natasha's wool was too coarse for the ladies who could afford to have someone knit for them.

Uncle Yozia and Aunt Zaya came to the rescue again.

They needed extra money, they said, and so they had decided to sell some of the things they had brought from Kharkov. However, they needed someone to do this for them and that someone was me. I was to keep half of the profits. I protested that this was not necessary, that after all they had done for us, the least I could do . . .

"Listen to me!" Uncle Yozia said sternly. "Didn't we agree that you were to listen to me as if I were your father? Well then, listen. We need your services. Can you see me selling one of Zaya's lipsticks? Or for that matter, Zaya selling it herself?" He pulled himself up with mock dignity. "People in our position in life? Unheard of."

"But——"

"But you will go to the *baracholka* next Sunday with Zaya's lipstick and you will drive a hard bargain. Remember that a fine lady from Moscow, or perhaps Leningrad, who needs a lipstick in Siberia, needs it badly."

"Why?"

"Why? How should I know? Am I a fine lady from Moscow?"

And so I began to trade on the *baracholka* every Sunday. A lipstick one Sunday, a bottle of cologne another, once a pair of slacks Uncle Yozia no longer needed. I enjoyed myself thoroughly. "This lipstick is guaranteed to be one hundred per cent indelible. . . ." "Kindly believe me. These pants will last a lifetime. . . ."

But when Uncle Yozia, having duplicate copies, asked me to sell a collection of Chekhov's short stories for him, I was not a good trader. I could not bear to part with it. I could not call out ". . . the greatest short stories ever written by a master storyteller . . ." I stood there mute, just holding the book up. I was surprised, though, at how many peasants came up to inspect the book. I knew they couldn't read one word of it—or anything else. Each one asked to hold the book, and felt the pages with frostbitten, rough fingers. I didn't know what to make of it. Was it a sign of their reverence for learning? I found it touching. The woman who did buy it looked embarrassed when I said that I hoped she would enjoy the stories. Well, I thought, someone—a child who has learned to read—will read it aloud to her.

I soon found out why the pages of the books were fingered.

A few weeks later, an old man held a book in his hands a long time, rubbing his gnarled fingers over the pages.

"Ah," he said, sighing, "this paper is too thin."

"Too thin for what?" I asked. "You can see the print clearly enough. And it is a wonderful book, *The Rain*, by Turgenev. If you have never read it, you will surely enjoy it."

"Don't tell me, child, that you think I will read this book?"

"Why else are you buying it?"

He threw his head back and laughed as if I had told him the best joke he had heard in years.

"What's so funny?" I was annoyed. "Books are for reading!" I wanted to add "you idiot."

"Oh, no, my child, not always. This one is for smoking."

"For *smoking?*"

He looked at me slyly. "But no, this one will not do. The pages are too thin for rolling cigarettes. They won't hold the tobacco."

"Good!" I cried, close to tears. And I yanked the book from him.

"Not so fast, child. How much did you say this **book** was?"

I doubled the original price.

The old man became furious and started shouting at me.

"But you said it was too thin," I shouted back, hugging the book to me.

The old man spat on the ground and went away complaining about me to the heavens.

And I went home as fast as I could, still clutching the book.

"My God," Mother said, when I told her what had happened. "Now we've come down to smoking books. First it was wrapping paper, then newspapers—now books. I hope the war ends before the people smoke up their libraries."

That idea was too terrible to contemplate. Books were sacred to me. For people to smoke them, page by page, chapter by chapter, was cannibalistic.

If books had become more and more sacred to me, it was no doubt because their high priestess was Anna Semyonovna. Anna Semyonovna taught us Russian literature, taught it with a passion and a knowledge of her subject that would have been extraordinary any place. She had been a professor of comparative literature at Moscow University and she did not regard the students of the seventh grade in a small Siberian school as being unworthy of her attention. On the contrary, she taught us as if she had gotten hold of us at the optimum moment for conversion.

She was very old and looked so aristocratic that I imagined her to be the mysterious survivor of one of the former feudal estates. Beautiful soft white hair, startlingly blue eyes, and skin of delicate perfection endowed her with a romantic past in my romantic eyes.

I topped myself in her classes and we became friends. Many times she seemed to be addressing herself to me, as if she understood that I had a special need. Perhaps I was right, perhaps she too had been sent into exile. It was in her classes that I finally mastered the Russian language and was able to read it with great ease and to write it too.

There was a price to pay for this proficiency. Anna Semyonovna singled me out to do a paper that I felt was way over my head and made me wonder whether she really was my friend. We were reading Pushkin's *The Captain's Daughter* and my assignment was to compare the historical facts about the bandit Pugachev with Pushkin's version of him. This meant doing research, and some original thinking.

"Who does she think I am?" I complained to Mother. "One of her students at the university?"

"Why not? You come from a long line of scholars, don't you? You're supposed to be a good student."

"Oh, Mama—"

But I saw that though Mother was excessively stingy with compliments, her eyes sparkled with pride.

I spent weeks at the library doing research and during that time the announcement was made that we were to have a students' newspaper. Since there was no printing press, we were to have a wall newspaper. That is, the contributors would write legibly, the articles would be pasted onto a board which would be hung up in the central hall, and the students would line up to read it. The editor was to be elected by the student body.

I decided to run for this office.

"You? Editor of a Russian paper?" Mother asked, incredulous. "Three years ago you could hardly speak one word of Russian."

"Three years is a long time, Mama."

"As if I don't know. It's an eternity." She shuddered. "And how many more will there be?"

At that moment, I didn't care. I wanted to be the editor of that paper. But my reason, my secret reason, part of an elaborate plan, was not journalistic; it was romantic.

His name was Yuri.

CHAPTER 20

A young girl's heart is indestructible. Perpetually hungry and cold, in the land of exile, I fell in love for the first time.

Everything about Yuri was attractive. He had curly black hair, gray eyes, and a gentle face. He was an upperclassman, and the girl he was always seen with—going to the movies, walking together in the village—was the daughter of the head of the factory and the belle of the school. She had an easy smile, sparkling eyes, and the most luxurious green quilted *fufaika,* which we all coveted. She had beautiful *sapogy.* She had Yuri. That girl had everything.

Mostly it was in the corridors that I saw Yuri and, at every possible pretext, I dawdled there in the hope of seeing him. And of being seen. But he never saw me at all. He didn't know I existed and it was to alter that condition that I longed to win the post of editor.

It was simple. I reasoned that if I were the editor, by some natural law of life Yuri would be a contributor and we would have to be in each other's company.

I finished the paper on Pugachev and to my pride but also distress Anna Semyonovna was so pleased with it that she read it to the upperclassmen as a model of what a paper should be like. As it was close to the time when we were going to vote for the editor and I was in the midst of my campaign for that post, the last thing I wanted was for anyone to be jealous of me. I wanted votes.

And I got them. I became the editor of the school paper. I didn't exactly win by a landslide. But all things considered, it was a sweet victory, particularly for Grandmother and Mother, who took it as proof that you can't keep a good family down.

Working on the paper turned out to be a pleasure. I enjoyed picking and choosing the articles, and I spent hours with Anna Semyonovna, who was faculty adviser for the paper.

But as for the editorship attracting the attention of Yuri, that was a total failure. Too late, I found out that Yuri had no literary aspirations whatsoever; his interests were purely scientific—math, physics, and chemistry.

Not that I regretted being the editor, but it did leave me less time for my new scheme, a rather shameless one.

I suddenly was overcome with a desire to improve my poor work in math. Special tutoring was what I needed, I told the principal, who couldn't deny it. Moreover, I knew just the teacher who could help me best, if she was available—a gentle woman from European Russia named Irena Maximovna. She was available and she would be happy to tutor such an ambitious young girl in exchange for my knitting her a sweater with wool she had brought with her.

So, three times a week I went home from school first, combed my hair, did everything I could to make myself more attractive, and took a long, cold, dark walk to Irena Maximovna's house, which, it just happened, was close to Yuri's house.

I never saw him there, and I began to seek assistance from fortune-telling cards. Natasha and Nikolay lived by them. Every night, they determined their future from the cards. Money, weather, health—the cards had the answers. At first, I looked down on this as amusing nonsense. But soon I decided that when it came to love, I was in no position to feel superior. Natasha taught me how, and the nights before I was due at Irena Maximovna's I too read the cards: would I meet my love the next day, would I not? If the answer was no, my desire to improve myself in math reached a low point, so low that I sometimes missed my lesson. But if the answer was yes, there was a great to-do about pressing my one and only skirt, freshening my blouse, and combing my hair.

Sometimes the cards were wrong, but often they were right. The law of averages, Father would have said. What did I care about such a law? Would it get me the attention of Yuri? No, my faith was in the cards. One day—one day, the cards promised it would happen.

In the meantime, while I was running after Yuri, another boy was running after me. His name was Shurik. He played the guitar beautifully, sang well, and brought me an occasional glass of sunflower seeds. He whittled knitting needles for me out of strips of wood, and with them and bits of wool I had picked up here and there, and saved from my knitting jobs, I made myself a pair of odd socks, all colors of the rainbow. He invited me to walk with him and his friends; he even invited me to the movies. Sometimes I went and sometimes I would refuse—for no better reason, I imagine, than that Shurik was not Yuri. Shurik and I were friends; that was all.

One day I was told to announce in the paper that there was to be a masquerade party at school.

"A masquerade party? In *Siberia?*" Mother was incredulous. "And what pray tell are you going to go as? A snowman perhaps?"

"Oh, Mama!"

At the word party, Grandmother's worn, sad face had taken on a soft glow, bathed by memory. "So it won't be a Venetian ball. Our Esther will make something or she will find something—"

But for me it was to be a Venetian ball. What first

217

real party isn't? I was as excited as any girl would be, in any part of the world. However, in the midst of the excitement I began to worry in earnest about what I would wear.

Then I got my brilliant idea. Notices had been posted on the movie house that a troupe of actors from a repertory company was coming. They would be doing Chekhov. I would go backstage and I would ask—very politely—to borrow a costume.

Day after day, I walked home from school never minding the cold and the wind as I daydreamed about a billowing white gown. I was not familiar with Chekhov's plays, but surely the great Chekhov, who knew all about the human heart, would not have neglected to have a character who wore a beautiful, billowing gown? And it had to be white. And a diamond tiara would sparkle on my head. (Mother had scoffingly said snowman; how amazed she would be to see her daughter dressed as the Snow Queen.) And of course the Snow Queen's escort would be the handsomest boy in school, Yuri.

A few days of this daydreaming and I became convinced that the gown existed and that all that was needed was for me to pick it up at the theater at my convenience.

And so with complete assurance—and a blue-red frozen nose—I presented myself backstage at the theater. A wizened little woman with beady eyes and pursed lips—not at all what I thought a member of a troupe would look like—wanted to know what I was doing backstage.

I no longer felt quite so assured. "I wonder—I

thought—could I possibly borrow a costume to wear to a masquerade party at school?"

The woman burst out laughing.

"I should say not! One of our precious costumes? Who in God's name do you think you are? What a strange, strange thing to ask for."

On the verge of tears, I wanted to say, But haven't you found out, lady, that when *everything* is strange, nothing *in particular* is? How is it you haven't found that out, here in Siberia?

I went home completely dejected. I had absolutely nothing to wear, and nothing to make anything out of, either.

"Mama, they wouldn't lend me a costume at the theater."

"The theater? You actually went there and asked for a costume?"

"Why not? I would have taken good care of it. And I asked very politely, too."

Mother shook her head, in a way that I secretly thought of as her Siberian head-shaking way—all disbelief. "To think what a shy child you once were—"

I didn't answer; but I knew that I was still shy—in some ways, more so.

I stretched out on my little bed with my feet up on the wall and concluded that life was a miserable affair and that I was the most miserable member of it.

"Why don't you see if Anya has something you could wear?" Mother suggested.

"Anya? What would she have?"

"With Anya one never knows. Run over there and

see. After all, she was the prettiest and most popular girl in Vilna——"

"So naturally when they banged on her door, she packed a beautiful ball gown with me in mind. Honestly, Mama!"

But I went to Anya's. Not that evening, nor the next. It wasn't that easy to part company with the Snow Queen. Nor with Yuri, who surely would not notice me in some old rag of Anya's.

After I had rather dispiritedly accepted Shurik as my escort, I went to Anya's. To my surprise, although she had not brought one of her ball gowns, she had brought a flimsy blue georgette with great billowing sleeves, the sort of thing she wore tea dancing in Vilna. Where had she expected to wear this in Siberia? I wondered.

As she shook out the rumpled dress and held it up to me, I looked at her. Poor Anya, Siberia had not been kind to her, either. Young as she was, working on construction jobs, going hungry—probably starving as much for her gay life as for food—she was beginning to look like an aging actress, a has-been.

I took the dress home and also shoes that Anya insisted I wear instead of my thick-soled ones. "You simply cannot dance in rubber-soled shoes," Anya had said. But how was I going to dance in shoes at least two sizes too large for me?

I tried the dress on and it collapsed around me like a parachute come to earth; in fact, I looked as if I had made an unscheduled flight and been left dangling in a tree.

"Oh, Lord—" I wailed; to have come to this from the Snow Queen was more than I could take.

Natasha and Mother circled me, trying to figure out what could be done to make the dress wearable for me without ruining it for Anya. The solution would be to baste me into it the night of the party: the collar, which came down to my navel, would be drawn into a ruff and the waist would be pulled in. And what would I be going *as*? I wanted to know rather belatedly.

"As something you're not," Mother said. Then she added, "In Siberia, you're always in masquerade—"

The night of the party, Shurik said he would pick me up at six o'clock.

"But Shurik, the party doesn't begin until eight. What will we do from six to eight? It's only one hour's walk to school."

"We will walk slowly. And we will talk."

And I will turn into an icicle in my flimsy dress and my thin coat, I thought to myself.

That particular night, the steppe was enchanted. A white moon had traced a pattern over the snow with millions and millions of brilliants.

Shurik took my hand. I slipped out of its grasp. He put his arm around me. I stepped aside.

When we arrived at school, the party was just beginning. I was trembling from the cold and from excitement too. Would Yuri ask me to dance with him?

No, this masquerade was not a Venetian ball. The costumes were less than glamorous. Here and there, someone wore a grandmother's old peasant costume or a jacket from World War I; some of the girls of the factory elite had been sewn into old crepe dresses.

But the belle of the ball was ravishing.

She was dancing in Yuri's arms, and she wore a beautiful red gown with fitted bodice and full sleeves and there were many petticoats under the skirt.

As she danced by, she left a hush of whispers in her wake.

"Where did she get it?"

"*Where* did she get it!"

"Well, *where*?"

"Didn't you see the production of Chekhov's *Cherry Orchard* last week? Don't you remember this dress?"

I stumbled in Anya's shoes.

So! When a little deportee makes a request it's strange, is it? But when the daughter of the head of the factory makes the identical one, it's a command—isn't it? All slogans to the contrary.

CHAPTER 21

That spring, the cattle cars came again, in an endless stream; this time, it was German prisoners of war they brought. All the goose-stepping arrogance was gone, beaten out of them; they were a bedraggled lot, hungry and sick. But to us, they remained monsters and we loathed them, all of us—deportees, European Russian, *Siberyaki*. All of us with reason; the stories of their atrocities were well known by then.

They were jammed into the same barracks we had lived in when we first came to Siberia, but very quickly new barracks had to be thrown together for the thousands and thousands who continued to come. Dysentery, cholera, and God knows what else killed them off like flies—and, as if they were flies, we didn't care. We had no pity.

Mostly, they were put to work digging ditches that were to be used for laying pipes to bring tap water closer to the huts, and for sanitary purposes too.

Each morning and each evening they were marched through the village in single file. And as they marched, every variety of hate was hurled at them, so that the air itself seemed charged with it. Garbage was thrown at them. Children screamed hysterically and threw stones at them. One little boy threw a stone that opened a deep gash in a German's face and a cheer went up. But all the time, the little boy was screaming, "You killed my father," over and over again. Almost without exception, the children of that village had lost either a father, an uncle, a brother, a cousin; sometimes, there were none left, no male relatives at all.

There were people who hid from these German prisoners, as if they were afraid that they were still capable of bestiality, as if it had not been beaten out of them thoroughly enough.

Some stood mute with their hate, their fists clenched with it. Grandmother, Mother, and I were among those. Silently, always silently, we wondered whether walking past us were men who had occupied Vilna, who had very likely plundered it, our beautiful city, who had possibly— The sentence would be unfinished; the silence from our family was a void filled with terror.

After they had passed, only then would I spit on the ground they had walked, only then did I have the courage to spit, and then I would also join those who hurled curses after them.

The prisoners shuffled along with their eyes on the ground, never once looking at any of us, never once showing that they felt the hate. They were treated badly—starved, totally enslaved.

That spring, the trans-Siberian railway, besides bringing prisoners of war, carried enormous quantities of booty.

When the tide turned, when the Russians pushed the Germans back into German territory and followed them there, the Russians did a massive retaliatory job of looting German homes, farms, and factories. Some of this loot was sent back to villages like ours in Siberia. Clothing, curtains, linen, silverware, all kinds of luxuries we had almost forgotten existed, were stored in a warehouse in the *novostroyka*. These things were distributed among the families of those whose fathers, husbands, brothers, and sons had been killed by the Germans.

On May 8, 1945, the formal surrender took place at Reims. The war with Germany was over.

That spring and summer was a violent time for the spirit: there had been deep sadness; and great joy; and then a tearless grief, some part of which would remain forever.

Only a few weeks before the great news that Germany had been defeated, there had been the announcement of President Roosevelt's death. We in the Polish community wept; we had lost our knight on a white horse, our hero who would save us. "Who will take care of us now?" Grandmother wailed. We had never counted on anyone so much as we had on President Roosevelt—and the United States Army—to save us from the Germans. "Who is this Truman person?" we asked each other. We had never heard of this man who was now going to be president of the greatest country on earth. We were afraid for ourselves and also we had truly loved Roosevelt.

Then came the joy over the end of the war. As far as we were concerned, once the fighting had stopped in Europe it was the end for us.

And then came the most terrible news of all. It came from survivors of the concentration camps, from their letters, by word of mouth, from the Red Cross. It came: all the members of my father's family—his brothers and his sisters, their children, his aunts, his uncles, his cousins—not one of them had survived the German massacre of the Jews. Of my mother's family, we heard that only two cousins and an aunt survived. My mother's brother, sister, her mother—my darling grandmother—her aunts and uncles, my beloved cousins, all were dead.

My mother tortured herself as she thought of the day she had told the Russian soldier she didn't know who the man at the door was. Perhaps if she had said that he was her brother, he would be alive.

Perhaps, perhaps, perhaps . . .

But we were alive. Our exile had saved our lives. Now we felt ourselves to be supremely lucky to have been deported to Siberia. Hunger, cold, and misery were nothing; life had been granted us. As Mother and Grandmother lit the kerosene lamps for our dead and said their prayers, I joined them in thanking God for having saved us.

One day, I asked Mother whether I might write to our caretaker, Stanislav, in Vilna. I wanted to know if the photograph albums had been saved. Now I had a deep hunger for them; I *needed* my past, my beloved past.

Mother said it was all right to write, but she doubted that I would get a reply.

I wrote the letter and I waited. Waiting, sometimes I evoked my own pictures of the past. A beam of sunlight coming through the curtains of my bedroom. The lilac tree in the garden. But I was careful not to people these pictures; it was too soon for that.

After some months, a letter came from Stanislav saying that nothing remained. The Germans had completely looted our house. No, there were no pictures, nor did he have any among his own possessions.

It was a crushing blow. All that remained would be in our hearts. If only Mother had let me take the albums that morning . . .

When the war with Japan was over in August, we received a letter from Father. He said he would not return to the village.

Mother said, "Thank God for that. Thank God he won't be coming back to this forsaken place. If he can only get back to Poland, then perhaps he will be able to get us out of here. . . . "

I did not join my mother in this prayer. I wanted Father to come back to the village, where I could be certain we would be together again. The thought of his making his way back to Poland—who knew how?—and of disappearing there frightened me. More likely than not, he would not be able to get us out and we would never see him again.

"Mother—why don't we ask Father to come back

here? The war is over. Life will not be so bad here. We have friends here. Why can't we live here? Please tell Tata to come back to us—"

"Esther! Don't tell me you want to stay here!"

She was shocked. And so was I. All my feelings and all my thoughts were a tangle of confusion. I was like some little animal that had been in the trap too long for freedom. I was like the people who had stayed behind in the mine to freeze to death. I was desperately, terribly afraid of change. Perhaps the thought of going back to a world no longer inhabited by the people I loved had something to do with it.

It was near the end of August when we had this first conversation about going back to Poland, a conversation that was to become a dialogue charged with emotion. The cubicle we called home was broiling hot; flies were buzzing all around us; our supper of watery potato soup was simmering on the stove.

And I did not want to leave this?

Well, I did love my school, didn't I? And my teachers. And my friends. And I suppose I had become used to this life. And I think that someplace inside of me there was something else—some little pleasurable pride that the little rich girl of Vilna had endured poverty just as well as anyone else.

I had forgotten what life was like "back there." Beautiful things and lovely cars and delicious food had become dim memories; life in Poland, even our home, had become a fantasy. Reality was here, in Siberia; I could cope with reality.

If Father came back here maybe we could make a life for ourselves here in the village. Maybe we could move to a nicer house in the *novostroyka*. Maybe Father could even get a job in the factory.

I tried to say some of this to Mother and she looked at me as if I had become a stranger, perhaps a traitor. Certainly not a political one, but in a tribal sense?

"Esther!" Her voice became shrill with disbelief.

Then I told Mother that I was afraid to go back, afraid to meet new people, afraid to live in a big city again.

"You foolish child," she said. "You are fifteen years old and you talk like a baby. What is there to be afraid of back there? What could possibly be worse than being here? Just let us pray that we can leave this God-forsaken place. I am sick and tired of it."

I looked at her. These words were written in her hair, the beautiful jet-black hair that was beginning to gray, the green eyes that were beginning to fail her. Even her teeth. She had contracted a gum disease and her teeth were beginning to fall out. Yes, Mother was sick and tired. She needed rest and decent food and freedom from worry; above everything else, she needed *freedom*.

And she needed Father. She was lonely for Father.

Mother became possessed by a wild, fierce desire to be free, to get back to Poland. She would lose her temper and scold me if I expressed my fears at leaving, my wish to remain.

Her tension grew when she learned that Uncle Yozia and Aunt Zaya were to return to Kharkov. Every day she would hear of another friend, another acquaintance who was leaving.

I tried to understand her unhappiness, but I prayed that some happy solution would be found for all of us. I didn't dare write to Father asking him to come back to the village against Mother's wishes. So I did the next best thing. I wrote short letters to him filled with expressions of the pleasures of living in Siberia: I told him how much more pleasant life was becoming, how much I loved school, how many friends I had. I told him that there was to be another declamation contest and that this time when I entered it, I would wear my navy-blue shoes. And who knew? perhaps this time I would win it.

Father wrote back that he was delighted that my life had become easier, but that he could not wait for the day when he would be released and permitted to return to Poland. His plan, his great hope, was that he would stop in Vilna—a part of Russia now—to see our home and then he would continue on to Warsaw or Lodz or some other big industrial city in Poland where he would start his life again.

Tata, too.

One day we received a letter. One glance showed that it was not from Father. It was another of those big, official-looking envelopes, the kind that sent shivers through us. Mother opened it and let out a scream! I froze with fear: the old cry—dear God, now what?

"We are going back to Poland," she said and burst into tears.

Mother who had been brave and strong, the Rock of Gibraltar throughout the years in Siberia, who had kept her sorrows, her loneliness, her troubles to herself, now wept like a baby from joy and relief—and perhaps some fear too of what was to come.

The deportees were to be sent back to Poland, but

not to Vilna. It was official and final: Poland, yes; home, no.

As Mother became more and more gay, I tried to hide my own fears, my own unhappiness.

"Imagine," Mother would say, "we will not have to plant any potatoes next spring and worry about getting them through the summer. Can you imagine how wonderful that will be?"

I tried to oblige Mother with my imagination.

"And if God is good to us, we will see Tata soon."

I joined Mother in that wish, fervently; the possibility of seeing Father again was the only truly bright spot in that unknowable future.

Presently, the first fearful step into that future was taken. Father wrote to us that he had been released from the brigade and that he had made his way to Vilna.

"Vilna!" I interrupted Mother, who was reading the letter out loud to Grandmother and me. "Tata went back to Vilna!"

Mother could barely continue; the tears began to drop down her cheeks and her voice shook as she read:

> Our house is still there and our apartment is in good condition. Much of our furniture is there too, but none of our personal belongings. I looked for photographs for Esther, but I could find none anywhere. When I rang our doorbell, a fierce-looking man greeted me: "Who are you and what do you want?" he asked.
>
> "I am Samuel Rudomin and I used to live in this house. I just came to see it and to bid it good-by forever."

"Well, bid it good-by and get out of here."

"And who are you?" I asked the man.

"I am the chief of the N.K.V.D. in Vilna."

And so, Raya and Esther, I left our home and I went . . .

Mother had to stop reading aloud and Grandmother and I had to read for ourselves that Father went to the cemetery outside Vilna to visit the graves of relatives and friends to bid them good-by. And then . . . and then he went to the places where some of our family had been massacred and he bid them good-by.

"I will try to get to Lodz," he wrote, "and I will write you from there. Be well and give my love to my mother. Take care of yourselves, for soon we all will be together and I want you to be well and in good spirits. This won't go on much longer. With love, Samuel and your Tata."

Father was usually reserved when writing, but this letter was filled with deep emotion. We wept for what he had written, and for what he had left unsaid. That night the three of us, Mother, Grandmother, and I, wept for our dead.

Little by little, I tried to begin to adjust to the great new upheaval in my life.

"Mama, I would like to have *sapogy* to wear back to Poland, the elegant ones that those other girls wear here. And a *fufaika*, Mama, a green one. I would love to have that, too."

"For heaven's sake, Esther, this is not what they will wear in Poland."

"How do you know, Mama?"

Mama's face clouded. I could see that my question raised the disturbing one that even she could not ignore: what would the plundered, ravaged postwar Poland be like? Would it really be home?

"I don't know," she admitted. And then because she must have begun to understand my fear and that I needed help to work it out, she said: "Very well, Esther, perhaps you should have *sapogy* and a *fufaika*. But you will have to earn the money for it. We have nothing left to sell. If you can get some knitting and if you can be paid with rubles—not food—"

Sapogy and a *fufaika*. Knee-high, shiny leather boots and a green quilted jacket. They became my obsession; the magic garments that would make me invincible on the dark journey back from exile.

CHAPTER 22

The journey back began where it had first started, in the village square. Late in the fall, when the wind had already begun and the first snow already covered the stones that had been like hot coals that first day, the Polish deportees were called to a meeting. Those of us who were left, that is. Many were dead—of influenza and typhus, some of old age, some of their frailty, some of broken hearts. Those of us who were left gathered in a holiday spirit and greeted friends and acquaintances with the particular camaraderie of people who have been through a thing or two together and have survived.

This time we knew what we had been called to hear: the final confirmation and the details of our repatriation. We were told that the road back was to begin in March.

It would be our last winter in Siberia!

The excitement was enormous and I was infected by it. Momentarily, I forgot my fears; or perhaps in the hope that it would cure me of them, I gave way to an almost hysterical excitement at the prospect of the journey.

And the prospect of owning *sapogy* and the *fufaika*. It had been more than wise of Mother to consent to my buying them (if I had enough money); it had been inspired. I began not to care where I was going so long as I went there wearing my shiny boots and my green quilted *fufaika*.

I found work—and wool—and I knitted furiously, this time for cold, hard cash. Before he left, as a farewell gift, Uncle Yozia gave me some rubles which Mother allowed me to accept.

Sometimes Mother became anxious about the *sapogy* and the *fufaika*. Wouldn't it be more sensible to try to get some fabric and make myself a dress?

"But you promised, Mama! My coat is so old and so short and so shabby. Tata will think I'm beautiful in the *fufaika*."

She smiled and argued no more; she understood.

The schoolwork went on as usual. I tried not to think of how much I would miss Anna Semyonovna and my friends—Svetlana, Katiusha, Zina . . . and Shurik. I tried not think of what it would be like to start all over again—new school, new friends.

But when I walked the steppe, I could not keep from thinking about the city. I found that I had forgotten what it was like to walk paved streets, to walk in the midst of automobiles and trolley cars and buses, to be surrounded by high buildings. I had come to love the steppe, the huge space, and the solitude. Living in the crowded little huts, the steppe had become the place where a person could think her thoughts, sort out her feelings, and do her dreaming.

Feelings are untidy; beneath all the pleasurable excitement, I still had a deep fear of going back to a city.

In December of 1945, Anna Semyonovna announced that there was to be another declamation contest and that it would take place in *March*.

This time I was invited to enter it by Anna Semyonovna, this woman whose faintest praise was like a laurel wreath on my head.

I told her how I longed to take part in it, but we were due to go back to Poland in March.

"But, Anna Semyonovna, do you think I could sign up for it just in case—?"

She gave her permission and when she asked me what I would like to recite, without a moment's hesitation I said, "Tatyana's dream."

A second chance. I would heal a wound that was still painful to think about; this time I would not only have shoes, but *sapogy!*

And so I began to work on Tatyana's dream and this time it was to be a race with a train that would take me out of exile.

Shurik came to our hut almost every day now as our time together was running out. He listened to me recite Tatyana's dream; and he listened and he listened. He was a patient boy. And he also talked to me about his plans. His father was a colonel in the Red Army and when he was released, Shurik and his mother would rejoin him in Leningrad where they used to live. And there, Shurik would go to a military academy and become a soldier too.

"Shurik," I would say to him, "why do you want to be a soldier? Wars are horrible. Look what they have done to us, to our families. One people fighting another people, what's the sense of it? Shurik, why don't you be a musician instead?"

And he would answer, "But every country has to have an army and I want to be in mine. You'll never understand because you're not a boy."

He was right; I never did understand.

While I knitted, Shurik read to me. My eyes had become badly strained and I could no longer read and knit at the same time. Shurik read me Dickens' *Dombey and Son* and stories by Dumas. Dumas sent me into daydreams of beautiful balls and lovely ladies swooning over lovers. Dickens presented a different picture. Florence Dombey had had a rough time of it in a rough world, but everything had come out all right in the end—which I found quite comforting when my daydreams failed me. Dickens, Dumas, Jack London—they had helped me escape from Siberia and now they would help me on the road back.

The contest was scheduled for March 18, and on the first of March, we received word that we were to leave on the fifteenth!

I was heartbroken. To miss the contest by three days!

I bought my *sapogy* and my *fufaika*. Shurik went with

me after school. It didn't take long; I knew exactly what I wanted. The *sapogy* were black and soft and shiny; the *fufaika* was green and quilted. Shurik said I looked very nice in them.

Every night I took them out and tried them on.

Shurik came to help us pack (as if our belongings couldn't have been packed in an hour) and his mother sent some flour and half a dozen eggs for us to bake some cookies for the road. Shurik and I rolled out the dough together and baked the cookies in Natasha's oven.

And Anna Semyonovna sent for Mother.

Anna Semyonovna too wished to give me a farewell present. She knew how crushed I was about missing the contest and she wondered whether Mother wouldn't consent to taking a later train, if there was one.

Mother came back from that interview with her eyes snapping ominously. "Did you put Anna Semyonovna up to that? Do you think for one minute that I would miss that train—one I've been waiting for all these years? For your contest or anything else?"

"No, I don't expect that, Mama. But Anna Semyonovna thought she could find out from the police how long the transport would stay in Barnaul and that maybe I could stay behind and catch up with you there."

"Esther, you are mad! Completely mad! I wouldn't leave you behind for one second, not one single second. We are going to leave this place on schedule! and together!"

On March 15, 1946, we boarded the cattle trains that were to take us back to Poland.

I said good-by to Katiusha and to Zina and to Svetlana and to Shurik. I kept my tears back as we all promised to write to each other and to remain friends forever.

I said good-by to the steppe—to the wind and the snow and the heat and the monotony. And to its space that had at first filled me with so much terror and later had quieted and soothed me. I said good-by to the unique beauty of the steppe.

The cattle trains that carried us back to Poland had not improved with the years. But this time who cared? This time the cargo was so filled with joy—singing and laughing—that I forgot to be afraid of what was ahead.

Once again we traveled many weeks, making many stops. We never knew where the train would stop; but the names of cities like Barnaul and Novosibirsk had become familiar to us and it became a game to try to guess what the next stop would be.

And we never knew when the train would start, either.

We had stopped someplace in the Urals to take on water. I longed for fresh air with a longing that had become an addiction from my life on the steppe. Mother was asleep, so I dared to jump down from the train for a minute, slipping under the bar that stretched across the open door. (Doors were left open now.)

It was so beautiful there in the Urals. I took great, deep breaths of this marvelous air and I also filled myself up with the beauty of this untouched, unspoiled place.

The whistle blew. The train started to move. And there I was, all alone, admiring the Ural Mountains. Not a soul in sight.

But someone else had been hungry for air and beauty.

He was leaning out over the bar, admiring the view too. His name was Reiner. We had known him back in Rubtsovsk and Mother had done him a good turn now and then. No matter. He would have done what he did anyhow.

He jumped off the moving train, the train that was to take him back to freedom. Cursing me vigorously, he picked me up and threw me over the bar and back into our car. The train picked up speed as Reiner raced alongside it.

In the general commotion, Mother woke up. I wept terribly for what I had done. But Reiner's father sat quietly, not weeping, not saying one word of reproach.

The hours went by and they were ghastly. There was no possibility of communicating with anyone—the cars were separated from each other—until the next stop, and who knew when that would be?

There was no singing or joy in that car now.

At the end of three hours—by far the longest in my life—we made another stop.

Racing down the platform came Reiner. He had just managed to grab hold of the little ladder at the end of the train and he had hoisted himself up onto a tiny platform back there. It had been an exceedingly cold ride.

I don't know whether anyone forgave me or not; in any event, they went back to singing, louder than ever. I thought that Reiner's father was the most noble man I had ever met.

I decided to make no more personal stops.

But we were told that we were going to stop in Moscow and that we would have an afternoon to visit the city. I was thrilled. Anna Semyonovna had talked about Moscow so much that I felt I would know my way blind to the Square, to the Kremlin, to the Museum, the Bolshoi Theater, and her beloved university. As we steamed into the Moscow station, I was all dressed up in my *sapogy* and my *fufaika*, all set to be a well-dressed tourist.

Suddenly, the train lurched and the next thing I knew I had fallen against the belly stove which was in the middle of the car. Apparently, I broke the full weight of my fall with one hand. The burn was a severe one, the size of a large coin, and the seared and blackened flesh signified that it was a third-degree burn. Everyone became excited again, but there was nothing to do about it except wrap my hand in a handkerchief. I was in agony.

My tour of Moscow was indefinitely postponed.

When we crossed the border from Russia to Poland, everyone reacted differently to this—for us—historic moment. Some people burst into tears, some cheered loudly, some said prayers of thankfulness. Some said the Kaddish for those who had not come back.

And then we went back to singing until we stopped at the first Polish village. At this village, there were some Polish people who had learned nothing from the blood bath. When they heard that there were Jews in the cattle cars, they let out shrill catcalls, they screamed and they cursed and they hurled stones at the cars. "Who needs you?" they screamed. "Go back to Siberia, you dirty Jews."

We stopped singing. I remember someone in the car moaning, "Not again, dear God in heaven, not again."

And I said, "Amen."

I was frightened and I was bewildered. The Polish people whom I had idolized during the years of my exile, thinking that life among them had been the best that ever could have been, were screaming at us to go back. At that moment, I wished I were back there.

Our destination was Lodz. We took turns looking out the four tiny windows and the first person who caught sight of the city and the devastation let out a cry of pain. When it was my turn to look, I too was appalled. The streets and the houses were filled with rubble.

But I was going to see Tata and I concentrated on shining my *sapogy* until I could almost see myself in them, and brushing every speck of dust—and some imaginary ones—from my *fufaika*.

The train stopped.

Everyone in the car was ready to leave and we waited for the officials to give us permission to do so.

I took one last look out of the car to see if Father had received our letters and had come to meet us. In those days, such meetings were minor miracles; more ordinarily, one lined up at Red Cross headquarters or at some other agency to meet a father or a mother again. Sometimes it took months to find each other, sometimes years.

Suddenly I saw him.

He wore a well-cut dark blue coat and a navy Homburg. He looked so dear and yet so strange, like a figure out of the American movies I had seen in Siberia.

"Tata—Tata—" I squeezed through the tiny window and waved.

"Lalinka—lalinka—"

"Oh, Tata—Tata—" I laughed and I cried and I waved. "When are they going to let us out? Soon?"

Even from my perch, I could see the tears glistening in my father's eyes.

The last two or three minutes of my exile seemed like an eternity.

Father had been looking around. "Here they come." He pointed to the officials who were sauntering toward our car.

We were cleared and I am afraid I bumped into many people leaving that car, making my way toward my father.

It took a long time before we stopped hugging and kissing each other, we four who were left of our family.

Father stood back and looked at us—Grandmother, Mother, and me.

He had to be told about my hand.

"How thin you all are, how very thin." And then he turned to me. "And your clothes, lalinka— But don't worry, the first thing we will do is get you some new ones."

"But Tata—"

I stopped. Only people out there wore *sapogy* and *fufaikas*. They would not be the height of fashion in Poland.

I clutched my father's hand.

The years out there on the steppe had come to an end, our exile was over.

CONNECTIONS

CONNECTIONS

The Russian Revolution: The Soviet Union Begins

The Russian Revolution of 1917 was really two revolutions. The first, in February, overthrew the imperial government of Tsar Nicholas II. The second, in November, placed the Bolsheviki (Bolsheviks, or Communists) in power and was the origin of the Soviet Union. The second revolution is the one described in this New York Times *article from the time.*

Bolsheviki Seize State Buildings, Defying Kerensky[1]

Petrograd, Nov. 7—An armed naval detachment, under orders of the Maximalist Revolutionary Committee, has occupied the offices of the official Petrograd Telegraph Agency. The Maximalists also occupied the Central Telegraph office, the State Bank and Marin Palace, where the Preliminary Parliament had suspended its proceedings in view of the situation.

Numerous precautions have been taken by Premier Kerensky to thwart the threatened outbreak. The Workmen's and Soldiers' Committee has been decreed an illegal organization. The soldiers guarding the Government buildings have been replaced by men

---

1. **Alexander Kerensky,** moderate socialist revolutionary who served as premier of the Russian government from July to October 1917. He died in exile in New York City in 1970.

from the officers' training schools. Small guards have been placed at the Embassies. The women's battalion is drawn up in the square in front of the Winter Palace.

The commander of the northern front has informed the Premier that his troops are against any demonstration and are ready to come to Petrograd to quell a rebellion if necessary.

No disorders are yet reported, with the exception of some outrages by Apaches. The general life of the city remains normal and street traffic has not been interrupted.

Leon Trotzky, President of the Central Executive Committee of the Petrograd Council of Workmen's and Soldiers' Delegates, has informed members of the Town Duma that he has given strict orders against outlawry and has threatened with death any persons attempting to carry out pogroms.

Trotzky added that it was not the intention of the Workmen's and Soldiers' Delegates to seize power, but to represent to a Congress of Workmen's and Soldiers' Delegates, to be called shortly, that the body take over control of the capital, for which all necessary arrangements had been perfected.

In the early hours of the morning a delegation of Cossacks appeared at the Winter Palace and told Premier Kerensky that they were disposed to carry out the Government's orders concerning the guarding of the capital, but they insisted that if hostilities began it would be necessary for their forces to be supplemented by infantry units. They further demanded that the Premier define the Government's attitude toward the Bolsheviki, citing the release from custody of some of those who had been arrested for participation in the July disturbances. The Cossacks virtually made a demand that the Government proclaim the Bolsheviki outlaws.

The Premier replied:

"I find it difficult to declare the Bolsheviki outlaws. The attitude of the Government toward the present Bolsheviki activities is known."

The Premier explained that those who had been released were on bail, and that any of them found participating in new offenses against peace would be severely dealt with.

The Revolutionary Military Committee of the Workmen's and Soldiers' Delegates demanded the right to control all orders of the General Staff in the Petrograd district, which was refused. Thereupon the committee announced that it had appointed special commissioners to undertake the direction of the military, and invited the troops to observe only orders signed by the committee. Machine gun detachments moved to the Workmen's and Soldiers' headquarters.

In addressing the Preliminary Parliament yesterday Premier Kerensky charged the Military Committee of the Workmen's and Soldiers' Delegates with having distributed arms and ammunition to workmen.

"That is why I consider part of the population of Petrograd in a state of revolt," he said, "and have ordered an immediate inquiry and such arrests as are necessary. The Government will perish rather than cease to defend the honor, security, and independence of the State."

■ ■ ■

Siberia

James Clarence Mangan

James Clarence Mangan (1803–1849) was an Irish poet whose work was well known in the nineteenth century. In "Siberia" he describes a faraway, symbolic place he has never seen, but his talent as a poet gives the description considerable power. Some of the images are quite similar to Esther Hautzig's real-life descriptions.

In Siberia's wastes
The Ice-wind's breath
Woundeth like the toothèd steel;
Lost Siberia doth reveal
Only blight and death.

Blight and death alone.
No Summer shines.
Night is interblent with Day.
In Siberia's wastes alway
The blood blackens, the heart pines.

In Siberia's wastes
No tears are shed,

For they freeze within the brain.
Nought is felt but dullest pain,
Pain acute, yet dead;

Pain as in a dream,
When years go by
Funeral-paced, yet fugitive,
When man lives, and doth not live.
Doth not live—nor die.

In Siberia's wastes
Are sands and rocks
Nothing blooms of green or soft,
But the snow-peaks rise aloft
And the gaunt ice-blocks.

And the exile there
Is one with those;
For the sands are in his heart,
And the killing snows.

Therefore, in those wastes
None curse the Czar.

Each man's tongue is cloven by
The North Blast, that heweth nigh
With sharp scymitar.

And such doom each sees,
Till, hunger-gnawn,
And cold-slain, he at length sinks there,
Yet scarce more a corpse than ere
His last breath was drawn.

■ ■ ■

from The Diary of a Young Girl
Anne Frank

*Anne Frank (1929–1945) died young, but the diary
she wrote stands as one of the great classics of
World War II literature. Her experience as a Jewish
deportee in World War II recalls Esther Hautzig's,
but Anne Frank's fate was more tragic. The Franks—
Anne, her sister, father, and mother—chose to avoid
deportation by going into hiding in a back-room
annex in a warehouse in Amsterdam, Holland, in
July 1942. They were joined by the van Pels family
(the "van Daans" in Anne's diary), and Fritz Pfeffer
("Mr. Dussel"). All remained hidden until they were
betrayed to the Gestapo, the Nazi secret police, who
deported them in August 1944. Anne and her sister
died in the Bergen-Belsen concentration camp in
1945; her mother died in Auschwitz. In this excerpt
from her diary, Anne is writing to her imaginary
friend "Kitty."*

TUESDAY, NOVEMBER 17, 1942

Dearest Kitty!

Mr. Dussel has arrived. Everything went
smoothly. Miep told him to be at a certain place
in front of the post office at 11 A.M., when a man

would meet him, and he was at the appointed place at the appointed time. Mr. Kleiman went up to him, announced that the man he was expecting to meet was unable to come and asked him to drop by the office to see Miep. Mr. Kleiman took a streetcar back to the office while Mr. Dussel followed on foot.

It was eleven-twenty when Mr. Dussel tapped on the office door. Miep asked him to remove his coat, so the yellow star couldn't be seen, and brought him to the private office, where Mr. Kleiman kept him occupied until the cleaning lady had gone. On the pretext that the private office was needed for something else, Miep took Mr. Dussel upstairs, opened the bookcase and stepped inside, while Mr. Dussel looked on in amazement.

In the meantime, the seven of us had seated ourselves around the dining table to await the latest addition to our family with coffee and cognac. Miep first led him into the Frank family's room. He immediately recognized our furniture, but had no idea we were upstairs, just above his head. When Miep told him, he was so astonished he nearly fainted. Thank goodness she didn't leave him in suspense any longer, but brought him upstairs. Mr. Dussel sank into a chair and stared at us in dumb-struck silence, as though he thought he could read the

truth on our faces. Then he stuttered, "*Aber* . . . but
are you *nicht* in Belgium? The officer, the auto, they
were not coming? Your escape was not working?"

We explained the whole thing to him, about how
we'd deliberately spread the rumor of the officer and
the car to throw the Germans and anyone else who
might come looking for us off the track. Mr. Dussel
was speechless in the face of such ingenuity, and
could do nothing but gaze around in surprise as he ex-
plored the rest of our lovely and ultrapractical Annex.
We all had lunch together. Then he took a short nap,
joined us for tea, put away the few belongings Miep
had been able to bring here in advance and began to
feel much more at home. Especially when we handed
him the following typewritten rules and regulations
for the Secret Annex (a van Daan production):

> PROSPECTUS AND GUIDE
> TO THE SECRET ANNEX
> A Unique Facility for the Temporary
> Accommodation of Jews and Other
> Displaced Persons

Open all year round: located in beautiful, quiet,
wooded surroundings in the heart of Amsterdam.
No private residences in the vicinity. Can be
reached by streetcar 13 or 17 and also by car and
bicycle. For those to whom such transportation

has been forbidden by the German authorities, it can also be reached on foot. Furnished and unfurnished rooms and apartments are available at all times, with or without meals.

Price: Free.

Diet: Low-fat.

Running water in the bathroom (sorry, no bath) and on various inside and outside walls. Cozy wood stoves for heating.

Ample storage space for a variety of goods. Two large, modern safes.

Private radio with a direct line to London, New York, Tel Aviv and many other stations. Available to all residents after 6 P.M. No listening to forbidden broadcasts, with certain exceptions, i.e., German stations may only be tuned in to listen to classical music. It is absolutely forbidden to listen to German news bulletins (regardless of where they are transmitted from) and to pass them on to others.

Rest hours: From 10 P.M. to 7:30 A.M.; 10:15 A.M. on Sundays. Owing to circumstances, residents are required to observe rest hours during the daytime when instructed to do so by the Management. To ensure the safety of all, rest hours must be strictly observed!!!

Free-time activities: None allowed outside the house until further notice.

Use of language: It is necessary to speak softly at all times. Only the language of civilized people may be spoken, thus no German.

Reading and relaxation: No German books may be read, except for the classics and works of a scholarly nature. Other books are optional.

Calisthenics: Daily.

Singing: Only softly, and after 6 P.M.

Movies: Prior arrangements required.

Classes: A weekly correspondence course in shorthand. Courses in English, French, math and history are offered at any hour of the day or night. Payment in the form of tutoring, e.g., Dutch.

Separate department for the care of small household pets (with the exception of vermin, for which special permits are required).

Mealtimes:

> *Breakfast:* At 9 A.M. daily except holidays and Sundays; at approximately 11:30 A.M. on Sundays and holidays.
>
> *Lunch:* A light meal. From 1:15 P.M. to 1:45 P.M.
>
> *Dinner:* May or may not be a hot meal. Mealtime depends on news broadcasts.

Obligations with respect to the Supply Corps: Residents must be prepared to help with office work at all times.

Baths: The washtub is available to all residents after 9 A.M. on Sundays. Residents may bathe in the bathroom, kitchen, private office or front office, as they choose.

Alcohol: For medicinal purposes only.

The end.

Yours, Anne

THURSDAY, NOVEMBER 19, 1942

Dearest Kitty,

Just as we thought, Mr. Dussel is a very nice man. Of course he didn't mind sharing a room with me; to be honest, I'm not exactly delighted at having a stranger use my things, but you have to make sacrifices for a good cause, and I'm glad I can make this small one. "If we can save even one of our friends, the rest doesn't matter," said Father, and he's absolutely right.

The first day Mr. Dussel was here, he asked me all sorts of questions—for example, what time the cleaning lady comes to the office, how we've arranged to use the washroom and when we're allowed to go to the toilet. You may laugh, but these things aren't so easy in a hiding place. During the daytime we can't make any noise that might be heard downstairs, and when someone else is there, like the cleaning lady, we have to be extra careful. I patiently explained all this to Mr. Dussel, but I was surprised to see how slow he is to catch on. He asks everything twice and still can't remember what you've just told him.

Maybe he's just confused by the sudden change and he'll get over it. Otherwise, everything is going fine.

Mr. Dussel has told us much about the outside world we've missed for so long. He had sad news. Countless friends and acquaintances have been taken off to a dreadful fate. Night after night, green and gray military vehicles cruise the streets. They knock on every door, asking whether any Jews live there. If so, the whole family is immediately taken away. If not, they proceed to the next house. It's impossible to escape their clutches unless you go into hiding. They often go around with lists, knocking only on those doors where they know there's a big haul to be made. They frequently offer a bounty, so much per head. It's like the slave hunts of the olden days. I don't mean to make light of this; it's much too tragic for that. In the evenings when it's dark, I often see long lines of good, innocent people, accompanied by crying children, walking on and on, ordered about by a handful of men who bully and beat them until they nearly drop. No one is spared. The sick, the elderly, children, babies and pregnant women—all are marched to their death.

We're so fortunate here, away from the turmoil. We wouldn't have to give a moment's thought to all this suffering if it weren't for the fact that we're so worried about those we hold dear, whom we can no longer help. I feel wicked sleeping in a warm bed, while somewhere out there my dearest friends are dropping from exhaustion or being knocked to the ground.

I get frightened myself when I think of close friends who are now at the mercy of the cruelest monsters ever to stalk the earth.

And all because they're Jews.

Yours, Anne

The Trail of Tears
from About North Georgia

*The Cherokee Indians' rapid adaptaton to white culture
in the nineteenth century did not protect them from the
settlers when gold was discovered on Cherokee land in
Georgia. The Supreme Court ruled in their favor, but the
Cherokees were evicted from their tribal lands anyway.
They were sent to new lands in Oklahoma. The eviction
and forced march of 1838–39, during which about
4,000 Cherokees died, came to be known as the Trail of
Tears. The event is as cruel, if not as enormous in scale,
as the forced deportations of Jews like the Hautzigs during
World War II.*

Cherokee had long called western Georgia home.
The Cherokee Nation continued in their enchanted
land until 1828. It was then that the rumored gold,
for which De Soto had relentlessly searched, was discovered in the North Georgia mountains.

The Cherokees in 1828 [. . .] built roads, schools
and churches, had a system of representational government, and were farmers and cattle ranchers. A
Cherokee alphabet, the "Talking Leaves," was perfected
by Sequoyah.

In 1830 the Congress of the United States passed
the "Indian Removal Act." Although many Americans

were against the act, most notably Tennessee
Congressman Davy Crockett, it passed anyway.
President Jackson quickly signed the bill into law. The
Cherokees attempted to fight removal legally by chal-
lenging the removal laws in the Supreme Court and
by establishing an independent Cherokee Nation. At
first the court seemed to rule against the Indians. In
Cherokee Nation vs. Georgia, the Court refused to
hear a case extending Georgia's laws on the Cherokee
because they did not represent a sovereign nation. In
1832, the U.S. Supreme Court ruled in favor of the
Cherokee on the same issue in Worcester vs. Georgia.
In this case Chief Justice John Marshall ruled that the
Cherokee Nation was sovereign, making the removal
laws invalid. The Cherokee would have to agree to
removal in a treaty. The treaty then would have to be
ratified by the Senate.

By 1835 the Cherokee were divided and despond-
ent. Most supported Principal Chief John Ross, who
fought the encroachment of whites starting with the
1832 land lottery. However, a minority (less than 500
out of 17,000 Cherokee in North Georgia) followed
Major Ridge, his son, John, and Elias Boudinot, who
advocated removal. The Treaty of New Echota, signed
by Ridge and members of the Treaty Party in 1835,
gave Jackson the legal document he needed to
remove the First Americans. Ratification of the treaty

by the United States Senate sealed the fate of the Cherokee. Among the few who spoke out against the ratification were Daniel Webster and Henry Clay, but it passed by a single vote. In 1838 the United States began the removal to Oklahoma, fulfilling a promise the government made to Georgia in 1802. Ordered to move on the Cherokee, General John Wool resigned his command in protest, delaying the action. His replacement, General Winfield Scott, arrived at New Echota on May 17, 1838 with 7000 men. Early that summer General Scott and the United States Army began the invasion of the Cherokee Nation.

In one of the saddest episodes of our brief history, men, women, and children were taken from their land, herded into makeshift forts with minimal facilities and food, then forced to march a thousand miles (some made part of the trip by boat in equally horrible conditions). Under the generally indifferent army commanders, human losses for the first groups of Cherokee removed were extremely high. John Ross made an urgent appeal to Scott, requesting that the general let his people lead the tribe west. General Scott agreed. Ross organized the Cherokee into smaller groups and let them move separately through the wilderness so they could forage for food. Although the parties under Ross left in early fall and arrived in Oklahoma during the brutal winter of 1838–39, he significantly reduced the loss of life among his people. About 4000 Cherokee died as a result of the removal. The route they traversed and the journey itself became known as "The Trail of Tears" or, as a direct translation from the Cherokee, "The Trail Where They Cried" (*"Nunna daul Tsuny"*).

■ ■ ■

from Summer of My German Soldier

Bette Greene

This book is set in Arkansas during World War II. It describes the reverse of the situation experienced by the Hautzigs and so many others in Europe during the war. Here, a young German soldier has been forced to leave behind his family and home.

Walking back down Main Street with the bank bag heavy with rolls of dimes, quarters, and halves, I began wondering what I could do with the rest of this Monday. If only I lived in Wynne City, there'd be no problem. The public pool is filled with kids, more kids than chlorine; the school library is open even when school isn't; and the Capitol Theater has a matinee practically every afternoon.

A drab-olive truck, canvas-covered from top to sides, passed. I recognized it as the Army truck that had picked up the prisoners from the train station. It turned and angle-parked in front of our store.

Two men in Army uniform and wearing guns in polished leather holsters jumped from the cab. One of the soldiers, quite muscular despite a prominent belly, called to the back of the truck, "All right, out! Everybody out."

And out they came: young men. Two, three, four. Not much older than boys. Five, six, seven. Wearing their matched sets of blue denims. Eight, nine, and ten. As they walked towards the entrance of the store the backs of their shirts revealed for all the world to see the stenciled black letters: POW.

They were, with one exception, blond- or brown-haired and wore pleasant enough expressions. Didn't they know they were losing the war? That they were at this moment entering a Jewish store?

As I followed the last prisoner inside, I watched my father approach the guard with the corporal's stripes. "Something I can do for you boys today?"

"Yes, sir, Mr. Bergen. These prisoners been spending more time passing out in Mr. Jackson's field than they do picking cotton. So Mr. Jackson gave them two dollars apiece and the commandant said it was all right to bring them here for field hats." He pointed toward the one black-haired prisoner who was moving away from the herd. "Reiker there speaks American. He'll talk for them."

"Tell the boys to come over to the hat department," my father said as though he didn't hate them. As if he had never said, "Every German oughta be taken out and tortured to death."

When the nine prisoners were gathered around the counter the corporal shouted, "Reiker!" Reiker didn't look quite so tall or strong as the others. His eyes, specked with green, sought communication with my father. "The men wish to purchase straw field hats to protect themselves from your formidable Arkansas sun."

My father remained impassive. "Here are some styles in men's straws. These are the best quality at one dollar and seventy-nine cents. They will last you for years."

Last you for years? I checked out my father's face to see if he was making a joke at their expense. But it was empty of expression.

The Germans began trying on the hats, smiling as though they were on a holiday. Reiker had pushed out from the center huddle and was exploring the broader limits of the store.

One very blond prisoner turned to my father. *"Der Spiegel?"*

My father shook his head. "I don't know what you're talking about."

"Wo ist der Spiegel?" said a second prisoner.

Again my father shook his head. "I don't understand your talk!"

Voices called for Reiker, and at his approach the men parted like the Red Sea for the Israelites. Again the word *"Spiegel."* Reiker turned to my father. "They'd like to see themselves. Have you a mirror?"

Reiker used English cleanly, easily, and with more precision than anyone I know from around these parts. And he didn't sound the least bit like a German. It was as though he had spent his life learning to speak English the way the English do.

Again Reiker left the others to walk with brisk steps across the store.

The corporal was involved in selecting off-duty socks for himself while the other guard leaned heavily against a counter and rolled himself a cigarette. Neither seemed concerned as Reiker headed unobserved towards the door. He could be gone before they even got their guns out of their holsters. Terrified that the guards' casualness was only a cover for the sharpest-shooting soldiers in anybody's army, I closed my eyes and prayed that he would make it all the way to freedom.

But I heard no door opening, no feet running, and no gun firing. By sheer force of will I opened my eyes to see Reiker calmly examining the pencils at the stationery counter.

Stationery was one of the many departments seen to by Sister Parker. But Sister Parker was busy waiting on a lady customer, and lady customers take half of forever to make up their minds. Who was going to

▪▪▪▪▪▪▪▪▪▪▪▪▪▪▪▪▪▪▪▪▪▪▪▪▪▪▪▪▪▪▪▪▪▪▪▪

wait on Reiker? I wanted to, but I couldn't. I didn't
even have a comb. Why, in God's name, didn't I
carry a purse with a fresh handkerchief and a comb
like Edna Louise? I ran my fingers through my hair
and patted it into place.

I took a few hurried steps and stopped short.
Reiker may not wish to be disturbed, anyway not by
me. The skin-and-bones girl. But I can wait on him
if I want to, it's my father's store. Who does he think
he is, some old Nazi?

Pushed on by adrenalin, I was at his side. "Could
I help you, please?" My voice came out phony.
Imitation Joan Crawford.

Reiker looked up and smiled. "Yes, please. I
don't know the word for it—" Above those eyes with
their specks of green were dark masculine eyebrows.
"Pocket pencil sharpeners? They're quite small and
work on the razor principle."

"Well," I said, reaching towards the opposite
end of the counter to pick up a little red sharpener,
"we sell a lot of these dime ones to the school
children."

"Yes," he said. "Exactly right." He was looking at
me like he saw me—like he liked what he saw.

"What color would you like?" I asked, not really
thinking about pencil sharpeners. "They come in red,
yellow, and green."

"I'll take the one you chose," said Reiker. He placed six yellow pencils and three stenographic pads on the counter. "And you did not tell me," he said, "what you call these pocket pencil sharpeners."

He was so nice. How could he have been one of those—those brutal, black-booted Nazis? "Well, I don't think they actually call them much of anything, but if they were to call them by their right name they'd probably call them pocket pencil sharpeners."

Reiker laughed and for a moment, this moment we were friends. And now I knew something more. He wasn't a bad man.

"Could I ask you something?" I asked, impressed by my own nerve. His face registered the kind of flat openness that comes when you haven't the slightest idea what to expect. "Well, I was wondering how—where you learned to speak such good English?"

He seemed relieved. "No great credit to me." He showed fine, white teeth. "My mother was born in Manchester, in England, and my father was educated in London."

"Gee, that's something," I said, immediately regretting my "gee." "Being born in one country," I went on, " and then having to go clear over to another to get educated."

"Keep in mind the relative smallness of European countries. It's like being born in Arkansas and going to a university in, say, Tennessee."

"Oh," I answered, still feeling the grandeur of it. "What did he study in England?"

"History. He's an historian."

"I never met an historian. What do they do? Teach?"

"What is your name?" he asked, quietly.

"Well, my real name is Patricia Ann Bergen," I said, grateful that I was able to remember. "Mostly, though, my friends call me Patty."

"And my real name is Frederick Anton Reiker, and when I had friends they always called me Anton. So I hope you will too, Patty."

"O.K.," I said, feeling too shy to speak his name.

"Back to your questions." He sounded very businesslike. "My father is a professor at the University of Göttingen in Germany. Before the war he wrote two books and a great many articles, but not any more. Now nobody is allowed to write." Anton sighed as though he had just run out of energy.

"And did you teach too?" I asked, wanting to know everything there was to know about him.

Anton moved his head from side to side. "Before I became a cotton picker I was a private in the German Army and before that a medical student."

"Someday when the war is over," I heard the sound of conviction in my voice, "you'll go back to school, become a doctor."

Anton shrugged. "Someday—perhaps." Then with a grin calculated to banish heaviness he said, "I believe it's here in the cotton fields of Arkansas that I'm destined to find fame and fortune." My smile joined his.

"Yes," I agreed. "You and Mr. Eli Whitney."

"Eli Whitney?" Anton repeated. "Should I know him?"

I searched his face for fraud. Surely a man as smart as he would know what every third-grader knows. "Well, Eli Whitney invented the cotton gin; it sucks all the seeds out of cotton like a giant vacuum cleaner."

"Clever of Mr. Whitney. Perhaps even genius. What is genius, anyway, if it isn't the ability to give an adequate response to a great challenge?"

"I don't know," I said thoughtfully. "I'll have to think about that."

"I hope you do, Patty. Next time we meet you can tell me your conclusions."

A distant voice intruded upon us. "All right, boys, the truck is leaving. Let's go."

Anton took a dollar bill from a cocoa-brown wallet made of the smoothest calfskin. A fine wallet,

■■■

better even than our very best ones and they sell for
five dollars. I counted back the change.

"Good-bye, Patty."

"Good-bye, Anton. I hope you'll be all right."

As he turned to go, my eyes closed. I found
myself carrying on a silent conversation with God.
Oh God, would it be at all possible for Frederick
Anton Reiker to become my friend? I understand
that it's not an easy request, but I would be so grateful that I'll never bother you for another thing. But if
this is something you can't arrange, then could you
please keep him safe so that he can return to his own
country and become a doctor? Thank you, dear God.

"Patty!" Anton's voice. I opened my eyes. He was
pointing to some object behind the glass-enclosed
jewelry counter. "Sell me this pin. The round one in
back that looks like diamonds."

I followed his pointing finger. It was big and
gaudy, nothing that Anton would in a million years
buy. "Not this one?" I asked, expecting to be embarrassed by so obvious a mistake.

"Exactly right!" he practically shouted, as he took
the pin tagged a dollar, dropped the money into my
hand, and went off grinning a different, more jaunty
kind of grin.

■ ■ ■

Gorbachev Resigns:
The Soviet Union Ends

Francis X. Clines

*On Christmas Day in 1991, Mikhail S. Gorbachev
resigned as president of the Soviet Union, a position
he had held since 1985, and declared the union
finished. His economic and political reforms had
changed the character of his country so profoundly
that the old order could no longer survive. This
article is from the* New York Times.

Gorbachev, Last Soviet Leader, Resigns

MOSCOW, Dec. 25—Mikhail S. Gorbachev, the
trailblazer of the Soviet Union's retreat from the
cold war and the spark for the democratic reforms
that ended 70 years of Communist tyranny, told a
weary, anxious nation tonight that he was resigning
as President and closing out the union.

'I hereby discontinue my activities at the post of
President of the Union of Soviet Socialist Republics,'
declared the 60-year-old politician, the last leader of

a totalitarian empire that was undone across the six years and nine months of his stewardship.

Mr. Gorbachev made no attempt in his brief, leanly worded television address to mask his bitter regret and concern at being forced from office by the creation of the new Commonwealth of Independent States, composed of 11 former republics of the collapsed Soviet empire under the informal lead of President Boris N. Yeltsin of Russia.[2]

'A New World'

Within hours of Mr. Gorbachev's resignation, Western and other nations began recognition of Russia and the other former republics. 'We're now living in a new world,' Mr. Gorbachev declared in recognizing the rich history of his tenure. 'An end has been put to the cold war and to the arms race, as well as to the mad militarization of the country, which has crippled our economy, public attitudes and morals. The threat of nuclear war has been removed.'

Mr. Gorbachev's moment of farewell was stark. Kremlin guards were preparing to lower the red union flag for the last time. In minutes, Mr. Gorbachev would sign over the nuclear missile

---

2. **Boris N. Yeltsin** (1931–), first democratically elected president of Russia (1991–1999).

launching codes for safeguarding to Mr. Yeltsin, his rival and successor as the dominant politician of this agonized land.

Yeltsin's Assurance on Weapons

Earlier today, Mr. Yeltsin told his Russian Parliament that 'there will be only a single nuclear button, and other presidents will not possess it.'

But he said that to 'push it' requires the approval of himself and the leaders of Ukraine, Byelorussia and Kazakhstan, the four former republics that have strategic nuclear weapons on their soil.

'Of course, we think this button must never be used,' Mr. Yeltsin said.

Out in the night beyond the walled fortress as Mr. Gorbachev spoke, a disjointed people, freed from their decades of dictated misery, faced a frightening new course of shedding collectivism for the promises of individual enterprise. It is a course that remains a mystery for most of the commonwealth's 280 million people.

'I am very much concerned as I am leaving this post,' the union President told the people. 'However, I also have feelings of hope and faith in you, your wisdom and force of spirit. We are the heirs of a great civilization and it now depends on all and everyone whether or not this civilization will make a comeback to a new and decent living.'

Still Against Commonwealth

In departing, the Soviet leader took comfort in the world's supporting his singular achievements in nuclear disarmament. But even more, he firmly warned his people that they had not yet learned to use their newly won freedom and that it could be put at risk by the commonwealth, which he fought to the last.

'I am concerned about the fact that the people in this country are ceasing to become citizens of a great power and the consequences may be very difficult for all of us to deal with,' he declared, implicitly arguing that his union could have remained a superpower despite the cold war's end, which he helped engineer.

'We have paid with all our history and tragic experience for these democratic achievements,' Mr. Gorbachev said, assessing centuries of suffering across serfdom and revolution, 'and they are not to be abandoned whatever the circumstances, and whatever the pretext. Otherwise, all our hopes for the best will be buried.'

■ ■ ■

Esther Rudomin Hautzig

Esther Rudomin was born in Vilna, Poland, now
Vilnius, Lithuania, in 1930. In 1941 she and her family
were deported by the occupying Soviet Army to
Siberia, an experience she describes in *The Endless
Steppe.* After her release from Russia, Esther spent a
year or so in Lodz, Poland, and then sailed to America.
On the boat going over she met her future husband,
a concert pianist. They settled in New York and were
joined later by Esther's parents.

Esther Hautzig attended Hunter College in New
York City and has written several books apart from *The
Endless Steppe,* including *In the Park, A Gift for Mama,*
and *Let's Cook Without Cooking.* She and her husband
live in New York City.